Potholes Along Memory Lane

Dave Bailey

Cartoons by Mark Pie'

Evergreen
PRESS

Mobile, AL

Potholes Along Memory Lane
by Dave Bailey
Copyright © 2007 Dave Bailey

ISBN 978-1-58169-241-9
For Worldwide Distribution
Printed in the U.S.A.

This book is a compilation of articles by Dave Bailey which first appeared in the Salt and Light Newspaper, plus recent "revelations."

Evergreen Press
P.O. Box 191540 • Mobile, AL 36619

DEDICATION

This book is dedicated to my grandchildren,
Emilee, Michael, Gillian, Colin, and Katelyn.
May they grow in knowledge of
and service to our Lord.

PREFACE

This book is humor and satire wrapped up in one package from the pen of Dave Bailey. I've known Dave for over 30 years. He once interviewed me on his TV program in Philadelphia, "One Hour for Christ." Since then I have seen the work of Ranch Hope grow.

The Ranch ministry to help troubled youth now has four campuses; Dave's "Ranch Hope Radio" ministry is preparing to celebrate its 50th year sharing the Gospel; and the "Salt and Light in the News" newspaper ministry continues. The material within these chapters first appeared in that newspaper, but Dave has added some unpublished musings as well.

In our ministry of film, video and magazines, we see the need for challenging Christians and providing "apologetics" for the Gospel in all media.

Enjoy this book. I'm sure it will make you laugh and think because we all know about those "potholes" Dave writes about.

Ken Curtis, PhD
President, Gateway Films

INTRODUCTION

If I had to pinpoint one lesson, among all the many lessons my father has taught me in forty years, the lesson that has been the most important is to have a good memory.

Never forget that God loves you and to keep Him first in your life. Never forget to love your family. Never forget the many teachers and coaches who have impacted and shaped your life. Never forget the many mentors that have shared their experiences with you.

Never forget both the good and bad personal experiences from which you have learned. Never forget to stay humble and have the ability to laugh at yourself. Never forget to share what gifts and talents God has given you with others.

I pray that as you enjoy reading this collection of "memories" you too will remember this lesson, and will thank God for it (Phil. 1:3).

David L. Bailey, Jr.
Executive Director
Ranch Hope, Inc.

Do You Remember When?

DO YOU REMEMBER WHEN...
- ...colored TV was black and white?
- ...Sunday night hymn sings were held after Sunday night services?
- ...a soloist and other gospel singers in church were accompanied by an organ or piano (before sound tracks on tapes)?
- ...Easter bonnets were worn by all women?
- ...the Russians were the Anti-Christ?
- ...Mickey Rooney was single?
- ..."rap" was something you did with presents?
- ...the only Bible you had was the King James version?
- ...you could understand the words in pop music?
- ...closets were something that held clothes, not a place to come out of
- ..."insured by the FDIC" meant real security?
- ..."mother" referred to the woman who gave you life?
- ...a family consisted of one set of parents, children, and grandparents?
- ...a woman carried a *baby* in her womb, and not an *appendage* or *fetus*?
- ...a church bulletin contained the worship service and a few announcements (long before all those inserts)?
- ..."Onward Christian Soldiers" was not considered a political statement for war?

If you can remember even 50% of these, you will appreciate even more the words in II Timothy 4:3-4:

For the time will come when they will not endure sound doctrine; but after their own lust shall they heap to themselves teachers, having itching ears, and they shall turn away from the truth, and shall turn unto fables.

Religion Without Cost

Amazing grace is freely given by God, but it is not cheap. The traditional definition of grace is: "the unmerited love of God." Paul wrote, "We are saved by grace and that is a gift from God." Like any religious doctrine, grace can be pushed to the point of the absurd: God does it all; I have no responsibility.

Nowadays, it's sad that many churches hire people:

...to sing in a choir.

...to visit the sick, those in prison, and those in need.

...to clean the church and look after the property.

...to play the organ, piano, or other instruments.

Many churches hire these people to perform the ministry that their members often used to do themselves. Is it possible that the next step would be that Christians will hire someone to attend worship service for them? It would free them up for time with the family, work in the yard or around the house, travel, or whatever. After all, one or two hours on Sunday does conflict periodically with other personal interests.

Seem absurd? Things do have a way of evolving or devolving, as the case may be.

I'm here to apply for the position of
"SERMON SLEEPER."

Mom

It has always been interesting to me that the two most popular songs for our two most popular Christian holidays were written by a non-Christian. Can you imagine if Irving Berlin had been a gospel songwriter? Wow! In addition to "Easter Parade" and "White Christmas," he could have really blessed us with some hand-clapping, soul-stirring, gospel music.

Obviously, our holidays are much more than nice lyrics about snow and Easter bonnets. We have all been blessed by the great messages of our Christian anthems and hymns during the holidays. This is especially true of Easter. As I sing "He Lives," "Up From the Grave He Arose," or excerpts from the "Hallelujah Chorus," this year I will be very mindful of the one who first taught me about our resurrected Lord. It was my mother, Stella M. Bailey, who has gone on home to be with the Lord. Easter always takes on a new meaning when a loved one is part of the heavenly host. Mother was a good alto and knew most of the songs in the old brown hymnal by memory. Thank the Lord I didn't become an alto, but she did teach me to sing those beautiful old hymns with my baritone voice.

The verses in John 14 were the first ones she had me memorize. Little did I realize that, many years later, I would be hearing those very same words read during her memorial service. For all of you who have walked that road and remember a loved one, I send the Good News from the lips of Jesus in verse 2: "In my Father's house are many mansions. I go to prepare a place for you..." (By the way, I didn't learn that one in seminary. Stella taught me that, too.)

Dave Bailey

Making a Positive Statement

Recently a local newspaper included an article by a national columnist. She was upset by a commercial running on several cable TV networks. Basically the ad presents a positive message about having babies instead of abortions. As the columnist indicated, the ad was very well done. She said, "It put a catch in my throat when I see it."

Perhaps you have seen the advertisement. It was sponsored by the Arthur DeMoss Foundation. I once met Arthur DeMoss, who was the founder of a large insurance company. Money that he left to the Foundation has been used for various evangelical projects. The *New York Times* estimated that $20 million was spent for this advertising campaign. I think the campaign can best be summed up by its closing text, "Life. What a beautiful choice."

The columnist I have referred to thinks the commercial is good ("Great Madison Avenue stuff") but that the other side of the story should also be represented in the ad: "An abused child, part of a cycle of poverty, and a teenage girl from an abusive family who becomes pregnant by a boy who doesn't want her or her child."

Her point is that the DeMoss ads are too rosy, too positive about life. Give me a break! Can you imagine what would happen if the columnist's rationale were carried out in every area of advertising? How about telling the other side to high-powered automobiles, such as when they end up involved in fatal wrecks?

Can you see how absurd it would become? Every time I saw the ads from the DeMoss Foundation, I thanked God that someone was making a positive statement about children, families, adoption, and life. Unfortunately, that type of message is just too much for some columnists and others in our society.

Even though I don't remember you, I want to
apologize for any stupid things I may have
done when we were both much smaller.

Dave Bailey

Class Reunion

This summer I attended a college reunion. Now I am in the process of helping a committee formulate plans for next spring when we celebrate the anniversary of our graduation from high school. Time does march on.

At the college reunion, I renewed friendships with some people I had not seen or talked to since graduation. There were some surprises. First, many of the group looked much older than I thought they would, while some looked much younger. With few exceptions, the talkers still talked, the smokers still smoked, the drinkers still drank, the dancers still danced, and the braggers still bragged. There were some pleasant surprises, though. One of my buddies from our old wrestling team had grown by leaps and bounds spiritually, and we found more in common than ever before. A couple of classmates had been through some serious physical problems but were winning their battles and giving God the glory.

It did seem very strange, though, dealing with the heavy questions always asked at reunions, such as:

Did you remember when...?

Whatever happened to...?

Were you there when...?

Did you hear about...?

I was saddened to learn that two of our class officers had passed away recently and that more of the class had not taken the time to make the reunion. I was also saddened by the passing of time that took my youthful friends of the 1950s and turned them into grandparents now in their late 70s.

But that sadness was balanced with a deep sense of gratitude. I was one of the blessed who had returned, and one of the blessed who could still remember and enjoy friendships of the past and look forward to the reunion of the future. I was especially blessed by the friendship of my college room-mate, George, who also attended the reunion. We have been friends for more than 45 years, keeping in touch, visiting, and watching our children grow up. This relationship has been especially important to me because George helped cement my relationship to Christ. It was his witness that helped get me ready for the ultimate reunion—the one that will take place in heaven. Thanks, George. See you there!

Thanksgiving Past

Thanksgiving 1950 was one that I will never forget and always cherish. As I bowed my head over the turkey that Thursday afternoon, experiences of a special year raced through my mind. That was the year we moved uptown from Penn Street to Broad Street. Thank you, Lord!

I was thankful as a 15-year-old because we finally had a shower and a bathtub. Saturday night baths in a galvanized tub in the kitchen were a thing of the past. We also had central heating, which meant there was no more wood to bring in from the backyard, no more coal to be carried up from the bin in the cellar, and no more cold linoleum floors in the morning.

The move also meant we had an indoor lavatory, so it was goodbye to the old outhouse. That place was extremely cold in the winter and hot in the summer.

We also had no more turkeys, ducks, or chickens penned up in our backyard. Every Thanksgiving and

Christmas the Bailey family had raised, killed, and sold their fowl to many satisfied customers. Sometimes the birds would escape to the neighbors, something I certainly was not sad to leave behind.

And, of course, I was thankful to have left 89 Penn Street—the house that looked like something right out of *Tobacco Road* or a "Ma and Pa Kettle" film. Our new home was a blessing, and it was located right next to the town movie theater.

Of course 1950 is now a distant past memory. The old house on Penn Street has been torn down, and the uptown house was just repaired and renovated by its new owners. I have much to be thankful for this year and will offer up continued prayers for God's blessings. But for some weird reason, I also thank Him for the years with the galvanized tub, wood stoves, outhouse, turkeys, and the old house on Penn Street.

The Dream Team

Your young men will have visions, your old men will dream dreams... Joel 2:28

Behold! It came to pass that the Americanites were called upon to do battle with their adversaries in the foreign land of Barcelona. It was the quadrennial ingathering of elite competitors from around the known world. To face each foe, the Americanites trained and equipped their very best for fierce conflicts. Most feared of all the battle hardened troops of the Americanites were the "Dream Team."

Who could stand against their onslaught? Who could stop their fierce fast break or slam dunk on courts of praise? Selah! They would ravage all who dared try to mount up with wings as eagles, or walk and not be weary, or run and not faint.

From the Angolanites to the Spanishites, the Germanites, the Brazilites, and the Croatianites, wherever word spread, behold the Dream Team cometh. "A plague will be upon your home!" You shall not overcome the likes of the Jordanites, the Barkleyites, the Birdites, the Magicites, the Robinsonites, or the Gasuntites (God bless you!). Who dare stand in their way? More deadly than a plague of frogs, able to annihilate the first born of the foreign nations, thus did the Dream Team obliterate its foes.

Blessed are those who obtain the gold, for theirs is the kingdom of resentment. Blessed are ye when others shall revile and persecute you for being "the victors."

But, rejoice. Yes, I say rejoice, for great is your reward in the kingdom of commercial endorsements (my apologies to the Old and New Testament writers). Amen and Hallelujah!

Put the US Back in the USA

The United States is quickly becoming a nation of "us versus them." More and more emphasis is being placed on what divides Americans than what unites us. Both political platforms appeal to many different groups, and too often each group is really a self-interest group. An agenda is presented by management, another by unions, one for African-Americans, Native Americans, Hispanics, WASPS, cities, farmers, white-collar workers, blue-collar workers, teachers, the medical profession, senior citizens, yuppies, and so on. My major problem is not that each group does not have legitimate concerns, but that they do not seem to think of the impact their agendas might have on the nation as a whole. It is the "us versus them" mentality.

In the early church, this mentality became a real problem, especially in Corinth. Paul had to remind the early Christians of something that American citizens should be reminded of today. In 1 Corinthians 12, he reminded the self-centered that there is to be no division in the body. Obviously there is diversity, but the overriding purpose of the Church's mission was to bring unity. One writer has said it well, "There is no room for selfishness in a bucket brigade."

Paul wanted the Corinthians to have a concern for each other. He used the analogy that if one part of the body suffers, every other part is affected. (A toothache does cause distress in other places than the mouth). We in America must again be concerned for each other. An "us versus them" mentality ignores and neglects those in need.

Paul also admonished the early followers of Christ to take pride in everyone's success stories. In this nation today, we hear little about encouraging each other in our successes. To move the country in the right direction, there needs to be a focus on good things happening.

Finally, Paul asked the Corinthians to see their own personal role in the future of the Church. In a sense he was asking, "Are you part of the problem or the solution?" That might be a good question for every American to ask. I want to do my part to put the US back in the USA.

War

Where were you on January 16, 1991, at 6:41 pm? I was sitting in front of my television, watching ABC News, tying the laces on my sneakers to get to a basketball game at the Ranch. It was at that moment when a reporter from Baghdad made us all aware that this was the beginning of what was to be termed "Desert Storm." War with Iraq was underway. My mind raced back to another day, in December of 1941, when news was shared around the world that the Japanese had bombed Pearl Harbor. That was a Sunday, and I heard the news after returning from church and Sunday school.

While driving to the Ranch, listening to the car radio for further details about our planes over Baghdad, I couldn't help but remember when I was just 15 and visited my brother at Fort Campbell, Kentucky. He was a paratrooper, and I went to the base to tour my brother's barracks and meet his buddies. Word came on that summer day that the North Koreans had invaded South Korea. Another war, another time.

To be honest with you, I cannot recall as clearly what I was doing when we started our escalation into war in Vietnam. That seemed a more gradual process, and no date stands out as clearly as the beginning dates for the other wars I've mentioned. Of course, since Desert Storm ended, a second war in Iraq began on March 20, 2003.

Because of my particular age, I have not had to fight in any war. However, I did serve two years of ROTC in college, overlapping with six years in the Marine Reserves (1954-1960). Although not a hawk by any stretch of the imagination, I have strongly supported my nation's military personnel, even when I may have disagreed with the politicians or military leaders who sent them into harm's way. This probably came from the fact that I had three brothers and a sister who served in World War II, and I have always had a strong sense of allegiance to, and respect for, this country's military.

As a Christian who lives in America, I pray that there will be no more days in my lifetime that will be etched in our memories because of the start of hostilities on the battlefield. Until that time, I will reflect upon the words of Psalm 3:4, "I cried to the Lord with my voice, and He heard me from His holy hill." It would be easier to let despair and fear cripple us at this time. "O Lord, another war!" It is time for our nation to again, cry out to the Lord for peace. And when peace comes, we should give him the glory.

Influential Women

Women are becoming more involved in politics. A few preach it is the wave of the future and that women will clean up a rather dirty business. Men should encourage the involvement of women in the political system. Just think of the great leaders in the Bible who were women. We could really use an Esther or Deborah today. It would also help to find a Lydia.

The other day I jotted down a list of people who had influenced me up to the age of 17, all of whom are women:

Mother
Sisters
Aunts
Grandmothers
Neighbors
School principals
Sunday school teachers
Choir leaders
Organist
Teachers
PTA leaders
Clerks in stores
Babysitters
Nurses
Girlfriends (not the least)

Let's face it, women play a powerful role in our formative years. They have not only the hands that rock the cradle but also the hands that discipline, educate, heal, serve, and do much more. If women play such vital roles in these capacities already, we certainly need more of them in our political system. However, let's keep something important in mind—whether our political leaders are men or women, they need enlightened guidance from the eternal God. Women are also sinners with a fallen nature, as men are, and they too can abuse their power. It should be our prayer, as Christian people, that our Lord will place spiritual men and women in high places.

Dave Bailey

Courageous People

Most of us remember Anne Frank, a brave Dutch teenager who wrote a World War II diary that won her worldwide fame. If you visit Amsterdam, you will see a statue honoring her near the canal house where she and her Jewish family took refuge with sympathetic Christians during the war. After two years of hiding, Anne Frank's family was discovered, captured, and imprisoned by the Nazis. The young lady died in 1945 in a concentration camp at the age of 15.

Many stories about people who did rather courageous things have come out of World War II . Sometimes Jews protected Jews; other times Christians helped them. In Anne Frank's diary, she shared something that certainly has impressed many who have read it, "In spite of everything, I think people are really good at heart." Can you imagine what it meant for a Jewish girl in hiding for her life to be able to write those words? That is quite a testimony of faith when you think about all the circumstances under which it was written. But it is also full of insight.

When we begin to think that everybody is out to get us, that they are uncaring, unloving, self-serving, and inconsiderate, we can develop some really bad attitudes. Obviously the New Testament calls upon us to be realistic about people—to know that we are all sinners who need to be saved by the grace of God. But we can't spend all our time dwelling on the sinful nature of man. We should also remember people who give of their time, talents, and financial resources—people who work on rescue squads, volunteer firemen, church workers, social workers, those who work with Boy and Girl Scouts, those who coach Little League, and those who volunteer in the hospitals. Sometimes we forget that there are people who have learned that their

15

treasure is not just to be laid up here on earth. These people have other types of treasures, and those treasures are seen in helping others.

Maybe it would be a good thing for us to think of people in whom we can see positive attitudes rather than those who display negative ones. Let's remember the words of a young girl: "In spite of everything, I think people are really good at heart." Thank God for those we see practicing that type of attitude.

A Failure Is Not the End

Recently our local District Superintendent, Harlan Baxter, mailed this one to our office. It's from an article called: "Perfectionism: What's Bad About Being Too Good?" by Miriam Adderholt-Elliott, Ph.D. We all have those days when we feel like a dunce in the corner, but we certainly aren't alone.

Do you ever feel like a failure? Join the club. The following people never finished grade school, but it didn't stop them from achieving great things:

Mark Twain
Charles Dickens
Claude Monet
Isadora Duncan

The following never finished High School:
Mary Baker Eddy
George Gershwin

Will Rogers
Both Wright Brothers
Peter Jennings

The following have or had learning disabilities:
Tom Cruise
Bruce Jenner
Cher
Hans Christian Anderson
Nelson Rockefeller
Leonardo da Vinci

Babe Ruth hit 714 home runs, but he also struck out 1,300 times.

A studio executive once dismissed Fred Astaire with the opinion: "Can't act...can't sing...can dance a little." His Oscar was only honorary.

Walt Disney was once fired by a newspaper editor because "he had no good ideas."

Abraham Lincoln began the Black Hawk War as a captain, but by the end of the war had been demoted to a private.

Charles Goodyear had so many business failures he was sent to a debtor's prison. Later, he accidentally discovered the vulcanization process that revolutionized the rubber industry.

Lee Iacocca was fired from Ford Motor Company by Henry Ford II. After becoming Chairman of the Board at Chrysler, he bought Henry Ford's former house and moved in.

Needless to say, these facts make me feel much better. All of us, at one time or another, have failed in some undertaking. While speaking to the young men at the Ranch last Sunday, I closed with this story:

A small boy was fishing and an elderly gentleman was standing next to him as they both cast their lines into the water. The little boy asked, "Mister, if I fall into this water, will I drown?" The older gentleman quickly replied, "Nope." Three more times the little guy asked the question, and each time the older companion responded negatively. Finally the little fellow said, "Why?" The old man wisely counseled the youth, "It's not falling in the water that drowns us; it's the staying under."

Rests

If you know anything about music, you'll know that there is something called a rest. It is a pause between musical notes. The rest is an important part of music, whether it is part of the rhythm of a piano composition, saxophone, or voice. Just as we need to have rests in music, we also need them in life. We cannot go forever without pauses.

John Ruskin once wrote about the spiritual implication of rest: "There is no music in a rest, but there is the making of music in the rest." In our life's melody, the music is broken off here and there by rests, and we foolishly think that we have come to the end of a tune. But it is just a rest.

Out of design, God writes the music of our lives. But we must learn the timing and not be dismayed or discouraged when God puts some rests in our lives. We need them. They are not to be slurred over or omitted, nor are they to destroy the melody or change the keynote. Every life needs its rest, just as music does. There are times when we get anxious because we can be too busy and forget about the rests in life. Enjoy some of them today. It will help you overcome a great deal of anxiety.

God's Hall of Fame

Sports fan that I am, I found myself glued to the TV for the final game of the NBA playoffs between the LA Lakers, led by "Magic" Johnson, and the Chicago Bulls, led by Michael Jordan. After the Bulls won the final game, I sat waiting for the TV wrap-up, and of course, the traditional visit to the locker rooms. My son and I were amazed to see Michael Jordan fall to his knees in the locker room. At first I thought he had collapsed from sheer exhaustion, but soon the other players surrounded Michael, and it became obvious that they were praying. In fact, if you listened intently, you could hear the Lord's Prayer being recited. It seemed that the TV crew was taken by surprise and was not ready for this reaction of religious gratitude. They made no comment, either out of respect for the moment, or because of their total surprise. Like many spiritual things in our society today, the entire incident was ignored.

Many people today believe athletes are overpaid and overrated egomaniacs, but that was not the case in the locker room that evening. It reminded me of the words of the Doxology, "Praise God from Whom All Blessings Flow."

Athletes, like all of us, must recognize their mortality

and that they cannot be on top forever. Bobby Richardson quoted something called "God's Hall of Fame" years ago on a Gospel radio program. It reads like this:

Your name may not appear down here
In this world's Hall of Fame.
In fact, you may be so unknown
That no one knows your name.
The trophies and the headlines and the flashbulbs here
May pass you by—and neon lights of blue—
But if you love and serve the Lord,
Then I have news for you.
This Hall of Fame is only good
As long as time shall be;
Keep in mind that God's Hall of Fame is for eternity.

This crowd on earth, they soon forget
The heroes of the past.
They cheer like mad until you fall,
And that's how long you last;
But in God's Hall of Fame, by just believing in His Son,
Inscribed, you'll find your name.

I tell you, friends, I wouldn't trade
My name, however small,
That's written there beyond the stars
In the Celestial Hall.
For every famous name on earth,
Or glory that they share.
I'd rather be an unknown here—
And have my name up there.

This puts everything in perspective for us, whether we

are an athlete, a professional person, a laborer, preacher, or a housewife. Fame and fortune do come and go. We must hold onto that which is eternal.

Belated Father's Day Greetings!

With all the excitement of graduations, weddings, and vacations during June, it is possible that Father's Day may be pushed down on our list of priorities. In fact, my daughter Liz called me the other night and wanted to know what I wanted to do on Father's Day. I was not prepared to answer. Somehow I had forgotten my big day! Just think, I have been a father for nearly 50 years, and I had no plan to celebrate. After more than 30 years of celebrating the experience of fatherhood, I was not prepared to tell my daughter what I wanted to do on my day.

Many of our boys at Ranch Hope have never known a father. Tragically, many men have aborted their responsibility to "bring them up in the knowledge and admonition of the Lord" (Eph. 6:4). A modern translation (NIV) says, "Father, do not exasperate your children. Instead, bring them up in the training and instruction of the Lord." It's quite a challenge and responsibility. So as we are honored on Father's Day each year, let's take our position in the family seriously.

By the way, for all of you who received ties you will never wear, cologne you think stinks, socks that are too loud, or shirts that don't fit—think of the love that motivated the purchase, and love the giver more than the gift!

Happy Anniversary!

This is the year of the 50s. Our radio broadcast celebrates its 50th anniversary, and Eileen and I have been married 50 years. While pondering these 50 years of history, I began to think of firsts that happened so many years ago.

For instance:

The first donation to our Ranch for boys—$20 from an insurance man in Bridgeton, New Jersey (I had asked for $20,000).

First name of the Ranch—Garden State Home for Boys (thank the Lord that didn't stick!).

First site that we couldn't buy—A 100-acre tract of wooded land in Aldine, New Jersey, owned by 14 people. They could never decide how much to charge.

First boy at the Ranch—John Sperry, who stayed just six weeks and left. We have never heard from him since. (He would be 50+ now.)

First teacher at the Ranch—A retired teacher from Woodstown, New Jersey, Mrs. Hitchner. We provided no books, no materials, and no classroom. She lasted one month and afterwards volunteered to teach in the Amazon at the age of seventy!

First cook at the Ranch—We called her "One Pot." She could cook an entire meal and dirty just one pot. It saved her from washing pots and pans.

First horse at the Ranch—Prince, a young stallion, who died at age 37 (99 in human years). Howard Gruber helped me break the colt before it broke me. Prince is now buried at the Ranch Chapel.

First success story—Mike is a real success story, and we still praise God that he came to us.

First full-time houseparents—The Denekas came down from Dunellan, New Jersey, and received combat pay after replacing the Turners, who replaced Harry Hess, who replaced Jim Bracken, who replaced the wife and me.

Thank the Lord we have followed the teaching of Jesus: "Seek ye *first* the Kingdom of God" (Matthew 6:33 emphasis added). It helps all the other firsts make sense.

Public Prayer

It is interesting to note what is happening with prayer at graduations and baccalaureate services. Our society and especially the school system in many states have become almost paranoid about the word *God*. It almost seems as if it is easier to get away with saying *damn* than it is saying *God*. It is easier to use the name *Jesus Christ* in anger or as a curse word than it is to make reference to Him in history.

The following is a tragic sequence of events that has occurred in community after community across our nation.

Step One – Limit reading from the Bible in public school. "No New Testament, just Old Testament. Read especially from Psalms and Proverbs" to prevent non-Christian religions from being offended.

Step Two – No Bible reading, either Old Testament or New Testament

Step Three – Prayer – no reference to Jesus Christ

Step Four – No Lord's Prayer

Step Five – No prayer before classes or other functions during school

Step Six – No reference to Jesus Christ during prayers at graduation or at Baccalaureate

Step Seven – No prayer at graduation; no benediction or invocation

Step Eight – No Baccalaureate services

Step Nine – No reference to God at graduation

Those of us in the Church who are concerned for society, and especially for our young people, should voice our opinion that the "separation of church and state" has now come to mean something entirely different than what our forefathers intended.

Imagine This One

Imagine the following news article:

**The Commandment, "Thou Shalt Not Steal"
Has Come Under Fire.**

The Presidential candidates have decided to take on something less controversial than family values. Politicians all state in a TV ad that it is morally wrong to steal, but little do they realize the firestorm that will erupt. "Closet Stealers" surfaced and thought they were being singled out.

Stealers Rights Group were next to voice outrage. "If we choose an alternate lifestyle, who are these candidates to tell us we are morally wrong?" They plan a march on Washington to influence Congress

to do away with all discriminating legislation against "stealers."

Freedom of Choice advocates have been very vocal. Appearing on CNN and Ted Koppel, two proponents of this group stated, "Choice, freedom of choice—a stealer has the right to do with his or her body as he or she wishes. We think it is another indication of the far right fundamentalists in our nation putting pressure on the candidates." They wanted, however, to make it clear that they were not advocating stealing, just the right that people would have to choose.

Various religious groups have also become involved. Some are upset that the candidates referred to the Bible as a standard. One church leader stated: "Stealers should not be put on a guilt trip because Moses thought he was being spoken to by God...this attitude toward stealing is a reflection of the morality of early Judaism and does not necessarily apply today...good biblical exegesis could show that Moses is really stating his cultural bias."

Sociologists have been quick to state that the candidates were raised in a culture where it was not necessary to steal. They had never known the deprivation that many stealers know. One spokesman angrily stated, "Those Ivory Tower politicians don't know what it is like to go hungry or be cold or homeless. They have never been driven to the brink...to stealing."

At the time of this writing, the TV ads have been cancelled and a new strategy is being planned that would be less controversial. As we go to press, the ACLU is representing one harassed "stealer" in a test case before the Supreme Court. As would be expected, the National Association of Evangelicals and the National Religious Broadcasters support the Bible, the candidates' position against stealing, Moses, and the much-maligned Commandment. Watch for further developments.

A Good Memory

Popular music always says a great deal about a culture. When I was a small boy, I would go up to our attic on rainy days and play records on the old crank-up Victrola. I especially liked the music of Al Jolson and songs such as, "I'm Always Chasing Rainbows." Of course later there were classics such as, "Rosie the Riveter," and "Mares Eat Oats and Does Eat Oats." By then, we had the automatic record changer, and I was enjoying "Blue Suede Shoes" or "How Much Is That Doggie in the Window?" Some of the lyrics of those songs almost make us appreciate Michael Jackson.

The Psalms of the Old Testament were the "popular music" for the Israelites. Long before MTV, these beautiful songs were a blessing to the Hebrew people. At Thanksgiving time, Psalm 103 gives us a thought that is often overlooked in our society. The author of the Psalm speaks of his personal relationship with the Lord. His music grew out of an intimacy with God. Verses 1 and 2 read, "Bless the Lord, O my soul, and all that is within me." It would be nice to again have songwriters with that mindset.

David reminds us in verse 2 to forget not all of His benefits. But there are some things that should be forgotten. Dot Worth, on one of her radio programs, spoke about experiences in life that can make us bitter but also better. Some experiences should be forgotten, but the Psalms remind us, "Don't forget God's benefits."

A speaker made me aware of this recently when he reminded me of the importance of the holidays. They are traditional times for us to be together as a family. I had not thought about it before, but our major holidays (Thanksgiving, Christmas, and Easter) are religious in nature. It would be tragic to divorce our celebration of the holiday from the religious nature of Thanksgiving—we are to be thankful to Someone, not some thing.

All of us at Ranch Hope send you these greetings from Psalm 103: 1-5.

> *Praise the Lord, O my soul;*
> *All my inmost being, praise His holy name.*
> *Praise the Lord, O my soul;*
> *And forget not all His benefits.*
> *Who forgives all your sins and*
> *   heals all your diseases.*
> *Who redeems your life from the pit and crowns you*
> *with love and compassions.*
> *Who satisfies your desires with good things, so that*
> *   your youth is renewed like the eagles.*

Dave Bailey

Christmas

All of us enjoy visiting with family and friends at the holidays. This year was an especially exciting one with one exception—a major exception—a visit from Rev. Ivan Odor and his wife. Although he is a good friend, I was not prepared for our conversation at a recent Christmas gathering.

He started off softly, but firmly: "We must take back Christmas. It is too commercial, too secular, too worldly."

I could sense he was angry, almost obsessed by his concerns. "This nation has moved far, far away from the silent night, the holy night, the babe in the manger, the story of a Savior being born." He became more intense with each proclamation. I could tell it was a subject he had often thought about. He continued, "I walked through the mall the other day. Santa Claus was the center of the festivities—there he was on his big throne, all the children and parents lined up to pay homage."

As he took a breath, I moved toward the dip table, grabbed a few crackers, a spoon of onion dip, and a glass of Dr. Pepper. I needed these resources to give me the strength to continue listening because I knew the Reverend was just getting cranked up. "Do you know I went from store to store in the mall and there was never a mention of Jesus—no reference of His birthday, not even a nativity scene, no Wise Men, no Shepherds. Whose birthday is it, anyway?"

Warming up to his subject, he continued, "How about the music? Who needs hip hop Christmas songs? Who needs Christmas rap? There was some awful music blaring out over the sound system. Just once I wanted to hear, 'Hark the Herald Angels Sing!'"

You know, I couldn't argue with him. I really knew how he felt. But I couldn't add anything to the conversation because the eggnog and Christmas cookies got my attention.

Trying not to be obnoxious, I carefully moved us toward the dessert table, and with one ear on Ivan, I dipped a cup into some eggnog and munched on an assortment of cookies while he continued, "And the people—pushing, shoving, dragging kids—were totally oblivious to the true meaning of this glorious holiday. What a fiasco—a plague on this celebration!"

With that, he grabbed his coat from our host's closet, threw it on with his fur cap and leather gloves, and started out the door. I was perplexed by his quick exit. "Ivan, why the rush?"

Ivan responded, "See you later. I just remembered some last minute shopping I have to do. The grandchildren changed their minds about their computer games. My wife gave me another list for the supermarket plus her personal wish list, and the church cantata is having its final rehearsal tonight. Gotta' fly..."

With munchies in one hand, I stood dribbling my eggnog, a question on my lips. "What?"

Happy New Year

I must get down to the serious business of making resolutions for the New Year. I am not getting any younger, and it is imperative to set goals, plans, and resolutions. After hours in prayer and calling out to the Lord, here they are. You can hold me to them. Not one will be revoked or altered as the year evolves. This year:

I will reduce the length of each of my sermons by ten percent.

I will have all new jokes and destroy those over-used and abused ones from the last 50 years.

I will pick up the phone once a week when my Caller I.D. reads "unavailable" and actually respond to a telephone solicitor.

I further resolve that I will try to sing at least three stanzas of the 15 stanza choruses in church.

I resolve to get a hair cut every four months.

I promise to stay awake on the couch for at least one night a week (and be good company for Eileen).

I will begin to sort through the many "collectibles" I have been saving that "will one day be worth a lot" and throw them away!

I will preach a series of sermons on the books of Leviticus and Numbers at Seaville Camp Meeting (by popular demand?).

I resolve to have less fun with my grandchildren and become a better disciplinarian, thus accepting my children's inability to raise kids.

And finally, I resolve to accept the fact that all of these have been broken by the time you read this.

Political Correctness

I want to put everyone on notice that from now on you are to be politically correct when referring to me. First, don't call me "white." I am not white, nor have I ever been white, nor are any of my relatives white. Maybe "pinkie" in the winter will do and maybe "brownie" in the summer. (Anyway, God is colorblind.)

Please avoid the term "Caucasian." It is a derivative of the word "Caucasoid" and pertains to the Caucasus mountain range (somewhere in Europe) and has nothing to do with me and little to do with my ancestry.

Avoid the use of the "homo-sapiens" label. It has too many connotations today, and some ignorant people may think it describes my sexual preference.

I become enraged (righteously indignant) when the description WASP is used. Do you really know what a wasp is? Have you ever been stung by one? It can be deadly! How can anyone be so insensitive and refer to another human being as a WASP?

While I'm at it, it is quite demeaning to call me a "guy" or buddy, and especially refrain from "hey, dude."

Political correctness must be a two-way or three-way street. Give me some respect.

Now for the hard-core matter: this term Methodist. It has to go. Do you know why this term was first used? It was a derisive attack on the followers of John Wesley. The group was very methodical. Wesley had a method for everything, so they called his church people "Method-ists." Just call me "united" and drop the other word.

And, of course, Christian is to be avoided at all costs. If you are a student of the Bible and church history, you know that this was sarcasm to the max. First called Christians in Antioch, the followers of Jesus were mocked because they were "like Christ." How can people be so insensitive and remind us of those disgusting days?

Now that you know where I'm coming from, please understand this is said in love. We PC people are only concerned with what is best for society. What I expect from you I will certainly practice in reference to you.

Date Setting

You may be familiar with the name Rev. I.B. Blessed. Rev. I.B. is a stellar detective and part-time evangelist who helps me with investigative reporting. At one time there were even rumors in Washington that he was "Deep Throat" of Watergate fame before the real Deep Throat was unveiled. Because of the nature of the most recent job I gave him, he solicited the assistance of Rev. R.U. Ready, noted "End Times" (Eschatology) expert. The nature of the investigation? The date for the "End of the World."

With so many people setting dates, I thought it only appropriate that I should give one too. After hours of intense study, the three of us have put our heads together and come up with something concrete. Here is the result: the world will end in 2035 on November 12 at 1:00 a.m.

Now for the rationale that led to this date:

First, no one else has chosen this date. It is unique.

Second, it gives most people adequate time to get ready!

Third, the Chicago Cubs should win their first World Series by then.

Fourth, most people my age will not be here to laugh and make derisive remarks if the date is wrong.

Fifth, if you add up the total number of chapters in Daniel, Joel, Malachi, and Revelation, plus John 3:16 (316), then multiply by seven (the perfect number), and then subtract 40 (a special number in the Bible) and finally deduct 666 (the mark of the Beast) you will arrive at the date of November 12, 2035. (Thanks to Rev. R. U. Ready for the math work.)

Sixth, and probably the most important, 2035 will be the 100th anniversary of my date of birth, and we all thought it would be an appropriate occasion for our Lord to return and wrap up this mess...

Grabbers

After trying to have a book published for nearly three years, I discovered an interesting phenomenon. Even Christian book publishers need a "grabber." They look for the extraordinary, the unusual, and sometimes the bizarre. So I have decided to do some new study and work on some material I think could definitely be published. Look over the titles and see what you think. If you have time, drop me a note. Let me know which book you would buy. It would help me know how to direct my talents. Here are a few samples of possible books (co-authored by my prestigious ghost-writer E.Z. Writer):

The Secret Life of John Wesley Revealed (Why he spent so much time on horseback.)

Are the Southern Baptists a Cult? (Former members give amazing revelations.)

John Calvin Plagiarized Martin Luther (It was predestined to happen!)

A Former Jehovah's Witness Admits He Was Coerced Into Going Door to Door

A New Gift of the Holy Spirit – Writing in Tongues

My Missionary Journey to Mars (Aliens hear the Word for the first time.)

I Broke Silence at a Quaker Meeting! (Excommunicated from the Society of Friends)

700 Club Scam – Now It Can Be Told (Pat Robertson Built Empire as Amway Distributor)

Making an Old Fashioned Mormon Marriage Work or How to Live With 12 Wives, 60 Children and 24 In-Laws.

The Rush Limbaugh Secrets of Marriage (Three Strikes and You're Out)

Ancient Dancing for the Stars or *Salome's Secret of Turning on a King*

Christmas Ideas
Borrowed from the book *Christmas Joys*
To celebrate Christmas...

Buy a pair of red flannel pajamas that you wear only on Christmas Eve.

Don't count calories from December 15 through January 2.

Never select a Christmas tree in the dark.

Don't give anyone a fruitcake.

Don't give your spouse a bathroom scale.

Remember the more a toy costs, the more likely the kid will want to play with the box it came in.

These were all nice, but my good friends Shark, Smiling Jack, Eutychus, and I thought of some really different Christmas joys:

In church, play the Chipmunks' tape of Christmas music for a prelude.

At home, roast some chestnuts on an open fire, deck some halls with boughs of holly, and take a ride in a one-horse open sleigh (just for old times' sake).

Give the latest in cookbooks – *How to Prepare Road Kill for Covered Dish Suppers*.

Take a shepherd to lunch.

Adopt an Amish family and pay their electric bill.

Here's a contest – have your church members try and guess how many times *It's a Wonderful Life* will be on TV between December 1 and December 24. Winner will receive a video copy of the original.

Try to find three wise men in Washington and send them to Bethlehem.

Be the One Who Comes Back

Someone said that there is a neglected holiday between Halloween and Christmas. Between the "rush" of Halloween and the "rush" of Christmas, we pass rapidly over Thanksgiving. I note there are very few decorations associated with Thanksgiving. Pumpkins, corn stalks, and mums are usually an autumn thing. Pilgrims, Indians and turkeys are usually confined to school, church, or the supermarket (not something we set up in the house or on the front lawn and decorate with flashing lights).

This holiday focuses on thanks, and thanks usually focuses on God. But I've always been confused by the number of people who attend church, either the night before or the day of Thanksgiving. I must admit that football games seem to win more allegiance than the local church. The statement is usually, "See you at the game" rather than "See you at church."

Of course, many of us use the family gathering on Thanksgiving as a great time to pray and say how grateful we are for blessings. But there is a part of me that wishes THANKS-GIVING was much more a day of worship and praise (less eating and football—more thanks).

Remember the Bible story about the ten lepers? We can make it very contemporary by saying "The 10 HIV-Positive People." Jesus healed them, and they went their separate ways. Amazingly enough, only one came back to thank the Lord for the healing. Hard to believe, isn't it? You would have thought they'd knock each other over trying to say, "Thank you, Jesus." Nine went on their way, expressing no word of thanks. Such can be human nature.

This Thanksgiving, I want to be the one who came back. I know you do, too. We need to thank Him for all the things He's done for us, things that demonstrated His love for us though they were undeserved.

On this holiday, there is no Thanksgiving tree to trim, no Thanksgiving lights to hang, no Thanksgiving carols to sing, and no Thanksgiving eggs to hide. But we have a life full of family, friends, and faith, not to mention "things" that cause us to go back to Him and say, "Thank you, Lord."

Generational Trauma

I am providing a public service for all who attempt to bring change to the Church. Hours in the library researching this material has given me a fresh perspective. I am also indebted to the notable church historian, U.R. There, Ph.D.

Below is a list of changes that churchgoers have had to deal with over the years. Can you picture what it was like for the first generation that had to face these changes in the Church? Here they are without commentary. Imagine the trauma for each generation that faced these changes.

The year was 1611—"I will now read from the new translation, the King James version of the Bible." One old timer gasped, "Modernistic Bible. Don't read from that!"

"There will be a special pot luck supper—bring your favorite covered dish!" Response by some deacons: "The Church is becoming a restaurant." (God be with you till we eat again).

"Next Sunday congregational singing will be accompanied by an organ!" One man said, "What next, soon they'll be having drums."

"Folks—don't call me pastor or brother or teacher anymore. Call me a Reverend." (A what?)

During the Middle Ages—"We're organizing a trip to the Holy Land, the place where Jesus walked! We'll call it a pilgrimage." (Don't they know there's a holy war raging?)

"We're going to start a new way of taking the offering. Put your collection in these little envelopes." (Now no one can tell what we put in!)

"No more baptisms in the creek, river, or pond. We are building an indoor baptistry." (It will never be the same.)

"Come to our church. We let ladies and men sit together on the same side." (What will this lead to—a sexual revolution?)

"Please hand out the bulletins. We must have order in the service." (What's a bulletin?)

Random Thoughts at Easter

Am I imagining things, or is the Easter Bunny taking over Easter like Santa Claus took over Christmas?

Recently, while on a major shopping spree in the mall, I noticed that Easter bunnies, chickens, baskets and chocolates are so prevalent that there is no room for an empty tomb or a cross. (At least at Christmas you can still see a manger scene now and then).

Peter Cottontail hopping down the bunny trail has replaced Jesus and the road to Golgotha (the Via Delorosa). As

Let's try it again. I say..."The Easter Bunny
has come." And you respond..."The Easter
Bunny has come, indeed."

the late Cardinal Spellman said, "America wants a Christless cross and a crossless Christ!

Remember when we used to sing "The Palms" on Palm Sunday? As a kid I used to sing, "O'er All the Way Green Psalms." To make matters worse, my mind also remembers a day I sang, "Up From the Grave, He a Rose." (Never stopped to think Jesus was not a flower.) Even worse was my murder of the English language and Christian theology: "I Serve a Prisoned Savior" – it's risen, folks, not prisoned Savior.

While we're playing "remember when"—remember when Easter meant a new outfit and a pair of Sunday shoes just for church and Sunday school? Remember that special time of looking for the Easter basket? I even enjoyed buying a $.50 tulip for Mom. Somehow it all related to the Savior and a celebration for Him.

The word *Easter* is in the Bible, but like so many Christian holy days, the roots of the celebration are secular. Maybe we ought to give Easter back to the pagans, along with Christmas, and instead make a new holiday and call it Resurrection Sunday. That way the Christers won't get confused. (Christers are those who come to church on Christmas and Easter). Calling it Resurrection Sunday might help people remember the great message of an empty tomb. It also might help us share the good news of eternal life for those who believe in Jesus. Let's start a worldwide effort! Or, on second thought, let's not! Just do what we've already been commanded to do.

Contracts

With everyone writing a contract today, I decided to pool the resources of my staff and come up with a contract for evangelical Christians. My trusted assistants, Rev. R.U. Ready, Dr. I.B. Blessed, and Mr. E.Z. Writer helped with this agenda.

It should be noted that for many years now we have been spending much of our energy on discussions about the following moral issues: abortion, crime, prayer in the public school, violence and sex on television and in the movies, homosexuality, and pornography. Below are some issues that need to be added to the agenda.

We wish Americans in the church would sign a contract to:

Fight against racism in and out of the church.

Spend more money and time on missions, especially in the Third World.

Do something about fallen preachers, priests, and bishops (like pray and help restore these fallen leaders).

Preach, teach, and live family values.

Start and support ministries for emotionally and physically impaired children.

Speak out against materialism in the church and paraministries.

Show more concern for unwed mothers and unwanted children (this is called abortion after birth).

Sunday School Picnic Revisited

Rev. I.B. Blessed and I were thinking back the other day (a definite sign of age). Our memories took a trip to the old Sunday school picnic held in the heat of summer, and we started playing the game "Remember When?" again.

Remember When...

...You couldn't wait to get on the old yellow school bus because that cute girl from the other class would be there.

...The park had an old cedar lake with a sliding board that proved our courage or cowardice. We'd dare each other to go down backwards.

...Rowboats could be rented for 50 cents an hour. Who had 50 cents? We'd pool our financial resources and hope that cute little girl from the other class would jump in the boat for a one-hour ride all around the lake.

...There was an old wooden building with a jukebox and pinball machine. Both were off limits to little Methodist picnickers, so that's where we hung out after swimming.

"Remember," I.B. asked, "the potato sack races and the great prizes? First place won you a pencil with "Jesus Loves You" written on it."

My favorite was the big softball game at night. The men would usually come over to the park after work, and we would have a knockdown, drag-out Christian softball game. It usually ended in an exciting takeout at the plate or second base. The combatants often would not speak for weeks until Christian charity healed wounded egos.

Wow, my mind also reviewed the memories of some

great picnic eating. The lady from the church (the one with big arms, black shoes, full apron, her white hair in a bun) always brought the greatest fried chicken, so I ate at her table.

The bus ride home was fun. We had a short devotional at the lake before boarding "Old Yeller." Mosquitoes loved young Christian blood and played vampire while the preacher gave us some spiritual food. I prayed that cute little girl would sit next to me but my buddy, Big Eddie, prayed harder. I missed by two rows and sat with Fat Bertha. So much for romance at the Sunday school picnic.

Singing on the way home was great. We started with 98 Bottles of Beer on the Wall, but that soon gave way to Jacob's Ladder, Do Lord, the Deacon Song, every Sunday school song ever conceived from "He Lives" to the "Hallelujah Chorus." Then, tired after a long day of spiritual frivolity, one by one we dropped off to sleep, only to arrive back at the church where it all started 12 hours earlier.

I looked at I. B.—he looked at me—and neither of us said a word. It was written on our faces: "Those were days of blessing. Thank you, Lord."

Debates

It is time to get our mind off CNN and think of heavier matters relating to the Church. There was a debate centuries ago about how many angels could dance on the head of a pin. It seems silly to us today, but history records such trivial concerns. Thank the Lord we have more important issues today to wax strong about. For instance:

For the record: Angels don't dance. We fly.
But if we did dance, it wouldn't be
on the head of a pin!

Was the world really created in 4004 BC? (Some Bibles say so).

Must we sing every stanza of a hymn? (Shouldn't the first and last be okay?)

Does the Lord understand the difference between a black church and a white church? How about a brick or white weatherboard church?

Why aren't there more sermons preached from the book of Numbers?

Why must the preacher "lift" an offering?

Was Paul's thorn in the flesh a Board of Deacons? (Or Presbytery?)

And finally, will the feminists make us close a hymn with A-women? (It should be A-men after a HYMN.)

More Debates

Recently my doubting friend Whoo Reely Nose and I were sitting on the beach thinking about subjects to debate. Some questions keep us awake at night. For instance:

Is Dr. James Kennedy a long lost relative to Ted?

Who does windows in the Robert Schuller family (especially at the Cathedral)?

Should Tony Campolo wear a rug (hair piece)?

Does Franklin ever take Billy Graham for a ride on his cycle?

Are Jesse Jackson's suits off the rack at J.C. Penneys?

Who perms Bill Gaither's hair?

Is computer whiz Bill Gates the Anti-Christ?

Did Benny Hinn used to do "Man From Glad" ads? (Remember the white suit?)

Is it a crime to use a handicapped bathroom like it is to use a handicapped parking space? Should special cards be given?

Are stretch limos getting longer at weddings?

Would you follow leaders named Bo and Peep?

In Remembrance of Dad

It's hard to believe Dad has been gone for 40 years. This Father's Day a number of memories surfaced.

Dad was born before 1900, and people were expecting great events with the arrival of the 20th century. Some even predicted the end of the world and the second coming of Christ. Into this exciting world came Clarence Salathiel Bailey. That's right, this isn't a misprint! My dad's name was Clarence Salathiel. No wonder they later called him C.S. If you think that's tough, I must tell you that Dad and Mom named their first-born C.S. II, and my brother named his first-born C.S. III. Today, Clarence II is called Clancy or Junior or Bale, and Clarence III is called Steve (after first being called Skeeter). By the way, Salathiel is a biblical name—he is listed in the genealogy of Jesus, and it is Hebrew for "loaned from God." Somehow I've always been thankful I was not the first born son (David means beloved of God).

Dad was a hard worker, a self-educated man, a good salesman, a people person, and a patriot. He formed a Boy Scout troop, was active in politics, was a member of the Odd Fellows, and he was a great Phillies fan. His occupations included everything from running his own candy business to selling chickens and eggs. He knew how to farm, hunt, fish, and put in long hours at DuPont. A strict disciplinarian, he was a good provider who managed to succeed in spite of two World Wars, a major national depression, health problems, six children, and one wife. In honor of Dad, I listed his favorite sayings that still make sense.

Don't let the door hit you (when leaving in anger).

I'll give you something to cry about! (if his discipline brought a tear)

Turn that radio down! (my own AM radio)

That's music? (when he heard my music of the 50s)

Get your hair cut (with the introduction of the D.A.).

A place for everything and everything in its place (the tool shed)

The teacher is always right (philosophy for education).

THINK! (Prizewinner for DuPont contest)

Don't drive so fast (when I drove the truck).

Take all you want, but eat all you take (mealtime favorite).

You should have had my father for a Dad! (reviewing the old days)

Never eat the part of the chicken that goes over the fence last! (great advice)

His favorite table grace for the Baileys was: "Dear Lord, please bless us. Make us truly thankful for what we are about to receive. For Christ's sake. Amen. (It's still used by my family and grandchildren.)

My dad was very supportive of my early preaching ministry. In 1958 he faithfully attended tent meetings at which I preached, and I believe in my heart he accepted Christ as his personal Savior late in life. Like Bob Hope (his favorite comedian), I can say, "Thanks for the memories."

Iced Tea Thoughts

Recently, I was socializing over a cool glass of iced tea at our local watering hole with my good friends, Rev. I.B. Windy and Rev. U.R. Lost. We were discussing some questions they have had to deal with in their ministry, questions that made them upset and almost carnal. I listened with great empathy and, after returning home, began to think of similar experiences I have had.

With pen in hand, I began to make my list of questions people have asked me:

From a layman, asking me to do revival services..."How much do you charge for preaching?" I responded, "You can't afford me!"

How long will your sermon be? My pat answer, "As long as it seems."

Someone asked me one night, *"Have I heard you preach that sermon before?"* Yes, actually it's the only one I have.

"Did you go to Cemetery?" Yes, I'm a Cemetery graduate.

"How come you talk so loud?" Genetics.

"Get some new jokes!" I need new writers.

Then, of course, I had to remember the caring soul who asked, *"Does your wife get tired of hearing you?"* Yes, actually she's not here.

The Lord knows how to keep me humble. Someone once said, *"Dave, we couldn't get Tony Campolo, so we're calling you!"* Thanks!

The following upsets me:

People who walk out with crying babies. People who stay with crying babies.

People who leave just before I speak. People who leave while I'm speaking. People who don't come because they know I'm speaking.

A graying couple who says, "You were our youth pastor in the early sixties!" (Not me!)

A preacher who asks, "Do you want to preach before or after the offering?"

Finally, a person who says, going out of church, "You really gave it to them today!" (I was speaking to him!)

Promise Keepers

Television personalities and programs such as Ted Koppel and Meet the Press were interested in a Promise

Keepers gathering in Washington, D.C. I was interested too. I have been to Promise Keepers rallies and have spoken at local meetings. "Stand in the Gap" invited men from across the nation to fast, pray, sing, repent, and be better husbands and fathers. Because of a previous commitment to speak in Lancaster, I could not attend. Dave, Jr. filled the gap for me. While listening to the radio and watching C-Span, I felt very much a part of the gathering. However, some of the criticisms I heard from various churches began to give me second thoughts. Here is a list of some of the more provocative. Various churches opposed Promise Keepers because:

> They gave out Bibles other than the King James version.
> They did not invite women.
> They are anti-Gay and Pro-life.
> They have a hidden agenda.
> They are too political.
> They are not political enough.
> They are anti-Democrats.
> They are too white.
> They are too Baptist.
> They are anti-Jewish, because they held this gathering on the weekend of Rosh Hashanah.
> Promise Keepers cry and hug too much.
> The founder, McCartney, is only in it for the money. (He couldn't make enough as a football coach.)
> They want this nation to be Christian and don't care about people who aren't.
> Men are to be the spiritual leaders in the family.
> This meeting was held on Saturday because no man would come on Sunday. (They don't miss pro-football.)

After hearing all this debated and discussed on radio and TV, I decided it would be necessary for me to call a meeting in Washington next month for us to repent for our negative attitudes toward Promise Keepers. It almost seems some people want "Promise Breakers." (So much for the popular press.)

By the way, there was one very positive note: PBS in Philadelphia asked five editors from across the nation what they thought. Every response was positive for Promise Keepers. I wanted to stand and shout "Hallelujah!" but my wife wouldn't let me!

Names

What's in a name? What's in a title? Recently someone asked me what my first grandchild would call me. I had never thought about it before. My friend then made some suggestions—Pop Pop, Grandpop, Grandad, and Gramps. Which one will it be? Now I having an identity crisis.

This caused me to visit my old friend, Rev. I.B. Blessed. He is my spiritual guru and invariably has an answer to all such dilemmas. However, instead of solving this problem, he introduced a new one—What do you like to be called in your vocation? I had never thought about it. I.B. Blessed said we have a number of labels to choose from. How about:

Pastor Bailey—sounds rural. Sounds like the farm. Sounds Baptist.

Father Bailey—sounds patriarchal. Sounds liturgical. Sounds Catholic.

Reverend Bailey—now this is getting closer. I note this means "one who is revered, entitled to respect, entitled to reverence." I think of Lutherans, for some reason, or Episcopalians.

Preacher Bailey—what a description of a vocation! There is no doubt what I'm about. According to the dictionary, "A preacher is one who advocates or inculcates religious truth." For some reason it sounds Methodist.

Clergyman Bailey—This is my least favorite. Checking with the root word, I found it originally meant "cleric," a learned person—the literate, to be distinct from the laity. Usually I am confronted by this one when someone doesn't know who or what I am. (Clergy includes priests and rabbis.)

Brother Bailey—now we are getting to the informal and personal. I feel at home with this one. Usually more conservative Christians hang this on me. Sounds Charismatic, Pentecostal, family-like. It also helps when they forget my first name.

Some other random labels that came to mind: Chaplain (this is usually from an ex-GI); Man of the Cloth (usually by those who work in the tailor trade); Doctor (for those exhibiting their education, only by degrees); Minister (makes me think of a Cabinet position).

Of course, my favorite is what the boys call me at the at the Ranch: "Rev." I can live with that after 40 years. When I preach they tell me to "Rev it up." I can do that. So next time you see me—just make it REV.

Sales

Across our great nation, merchants are having special summer sales. I decided to call my staff together and think of a way to help people get married—A MARRIAGE SALE—a reduction in costs to get hitched. We all know that today marriage is not cheap, nor is the marriage ceremony. We listed everything we could think of that is involved in a wedding: flowers, candles, special music, organist, preacher, gown, tux, invitations, reception, photographer, honeymoon, program, rehearsal dinner, gifts for the bridal party, rental of church, and rings. After making our list, my trusted staff and I thought of how we could cut costs for the couple. I called Rev. R.U. Ready, Rev. I.B. Blessed, and Dr. Ty A. Knot. Here are our findings on a summer SALE FOR MARRIAGE:

See if the pastor could marry more than one couple during your ceremony. For instance, if one wedding were $50 for the preacher, for four couples it would only be $12.50 each.

Have the service on the lawn or in the parking lot. People may remain in their cars. No rental or janitorial costs for the sanctuary.

Use flowers from a funeral service. Most cemeteries have flowers piled on the grave that should be re-used. If you feel guilty, take them back after your service.

Have a photographer who specializes in Polaroid pictures. Take as many as you want. You can see them immediately and save the later hassle of trying to decide which ones you like and want printed.

Have a potluck supper for the reception. Each guest will bring their own table setting and food!

Bring a Boombox to the reception for music. Do not hire an orchestra or a DJ. Turn on an FM station with good, middle-of-the-road stuff. Make it loud. No one will suspect what you are doing!

Do not spend money on buying and sending invitations. Call people and have them invite others. It will spread by word of mouth.

For your honeymoon, organize a tour. You and your spouse can be the guides. Remember, if 30 people pay to go, you will go free. Start planning on this one early. Avoid special rates for Bosnia, Kuwait, and the Sudan.

Promise pickup service for gifts, especially for those who can't come to the ceremony. Install a toll-free phone line so invitees can reach you easily and pledge their wedding gift.

I hope these ideas will help save you money on your wedding!

Confessions

Writing this section brings me a great deal of pain. The only comfort I have received is from my therapist, Dr. Utelit Ahl. He is a remarkable person who "feels my pain" and says, "Honest confession is good for the soul."

Let me tell you what precipitated this trip to the confessional. I read in the newspaper that a six-year-old boy had been suspended from school for kissing a little girl in his class. His act was considered by an educator to be sexual harassment, and he had to be corrected. At first I reacted with disdain for those who disciplined a child for such a seemingly harmless act. Then, upon further reflection, I realized I, too, was guilty of similar acts when I was that age. Below is a partial list of similar transgressions that my therapist was able to pull from my sordid memories. Healing has taken place, and I am no longer bound. Herewith are published names and experiences—any of the girls involved reading this, please consider forgiving me:

To Ronnie—for the Valentine's Day card in second grade that was suggestive about love and frivolous kissing.

To Lisa—for sitting extra close to you in primary class in Sunday school. The intent was to touch. Yes, to touch your arm!

To Margie—for passing those crude notes during school. I had no idea in third grade what x's and o's represented. The time I ran out of space on one note was a moment of delirious infatuation.

To Carol—forgive the episode in the choir room during Junior Choir rehearsal. I now admit watching you try on your new choir robe over jeans and a bulky sweater. Even though you were fully dressed, watching you was not in good taste for a little Methodist boy.

To Barbara—can you ever absolve me from the evil of picking your number 75 times during one game of Post Office? I admit that Spin the Bottle and Flashlight were promiscuous enough in the fifth grade. (In all honesty though, you were a good kisser).

To Michelle—a hayride to sing Christmas carols sounds innocent enough, but how it quickly degenerated. I think it was during "God Rest Ye Merry Gentlemen" or "Joy to the World" that I became aware it was very cold on the back of that truck. The hug was to stimulate Christian fellowship, nothing more. But I noticed you hugged better than the boys.

And finally, to Joyce—movie theaters are dark places and sitting with you was a manipulation on my part. Placing my arm over the back of your seat was not accidental. Holding your hand was intentional. It was cheap of me to ask you to meet me inside so I could save your $.35 admission charge. Forgive me my misspent childhood.

There! I feel better. Just seeing this in print is a catharsis. Fifty years later, I'm hoping it is too late to use this as evidence. Pray for me!

An Open Letter to Santa

Let me say up front that I have always liked you. From my very first remembrance of Christmas, you have been A-okay in my book. You never left coal in my stocking or switches under the tree (even though I often deserved them). I want to go on record that this believer has never been disappointed with what you packed on your sleigh or dragged down the chimney. Being from a big family and a depression baby (Mom and Dad were depressed), I have learned how to do without. During the big war (World War II), things were tough and gifts were small, but you still found your way to my house on 89 Penn Street in Pennsgrove. Through the tough years of starting the Ranch, raising a family, and living on a preacher's salary, none of us ever felt forgotten at Christmas.

When I think of your history dating back to St. Nicholas, I am grateful for your legacy of giving and caring. But Santa, Baby, something is going wacky. I want to make you aware of a grave concern I have. Please note:

To many children and adults, you have become Christmas! I know you may not like to hear that. I know you know that December 25 is a special day on the church calendar, a day in which we are to remember that "unto us is born a Savior, Christ the Lord." I know it's not your fault, but it's time to save Christmas and take it back from the pagans! Bring back the Baby, His mother and dad, the star, the shepherds, the carols, and the Magi! We need your help. Here is my plan:

Tell every child who climbs on your lap that God gave the greatest gift at Christmas.

Put a big manger scene near your throne at the mall, a subtle reminder for each family.

Use your original name—Saint Nicholas.

Tell the mall music director that you want more "Joy to the World," "Hark the Herald Angels Sing," "O Come All Ye Faithful," and less "Rudolph," "Jingle Bells," "Chestnuts Roasting," and "Frosty."

Pray with Rudolph, the other reindeer, the elves, and Mrs. Claus that the Prince of Peace will be left at every home you visit on Christmas Eve.

And finally, change your Ho, Ho, Ho to Ha, Ha, Ha...alleluia!

Lawsuits

Have you been following the recent legion of lawsuits filed against tobacco companies? If only a fraction of the money is paid out by cigarette companies to compensate "sick smokers," we are going to have a number of rich "victims" in our country!

I made the mistake of bringing up the subject to my mild-mannered clergy friend, Rev. R.U. Ready. He is deeply concerned about where this type of litigation could lead. "Suppose this mentality hits the church," he said. "Suppose every wacko who thinks he was victimized in Sunday school or by a preacher, priest, or rabbi starts to sue. Think of all the ramifications!"

I can hear it now:

"My bad back problem was caused by those wooden pews I sat on for 30 years. They were so uncomfortable! The church was negligent. I'm going to sue!"

"I became an alcoholic by taking Communion monthly. I should have been a Methodist; they drink grape juice, but my church had the best wine. I got addicted. I'm going to sue!"

"My kidney and bowel troubles came from using those terrible bathrooms in the church (or worse yet, the outhouse!) during my formative years. Church bathrooms were embarrassing to use. I held it till I got home. I'm going to sue!"

"The church caused me too much guilt—all this stuff about sin and evil and commandments and salvation. My time in the confessional also did me no good. My guilt complex is too much to bear. I'm going to sue!"

Hi! My name is Bob, and I'm an overeater.
It all started with my church's
potluck meals...

"My obesity is directly related to covered dish suppers. Sometimes our church held them weekly. Food was a constant temptation. I had to try all the special plates by each cook in our church, and now I have a weight problem. I'm going to sue!"

"My hip trouble and knee trouble come from the steps I had to climb to the sanctuary. No wonder I have arthritis—too many steps for too many years. I'm going to sue!"

I was really starting to get nervous. Maybe Rev. Ready was on to something. Suppose any of these cases found a lawyer. Suppose the lawyer was able to bring it before a judge or a jury. Suppose the judge and/or the juror had been victimized. Suppose they had been cut from the Christmas Cantata or the church softball team. Suppose they hadn't liked the way their baby was baptized or the way the new addition was put on the church.

The concerns were just too much to handle. I may go back and study law, pass the bar, and start searching for victims!

Church Music

While going through an old hymnal, I noticed how our music goes through transitions. Every generation or two, we sing new songs of Zion. For instance, do you remember any of the songs your grandparents sang: "In the Land Where the Flowers Bloom Forever" was quite a title to announce each Sunday. Another biggie (with flowers on our mind) was "Gather the Roses," a hit with the florist trade. Or consider this one for a board meeting: "Let the Meeting Go On, Let Me Die at My Post."

In an age in which the Holy Spirit is bringing revival, think back to this one, written in 1902, "Stay Then Insulted Spirit, Stay!" This title contains an interesting use of the word "insulted." Can any of you relate to this one from 1896: "I Was Poor as the Poorest" (refrain says "but the wealthiest of the world in Jesus")? If you have trouble with flying, James Rowe wrote, "I Know Who Pilots Me" or "Meet Mother in the Skies." Below is a list of songs you will want to file away. They might make a comeback in your church. If you want a copy of the music, write to me.

All of the following songs are from 1902:

"Behold a Stranger at the Door"
"I'm on the Shiny Pathway"
"The Fight Is On!"
"Lifetime Is Working Time"
"On the Hallelujah Line"
"Angels, Get My Mansion Ready"
"The Old Account Was Settled'
"There's a Shout in the Camp"
"I Didn't Stay Away"
"I'll Be Saved but Not Tonight!"

And how about: "Keep the Foe Retreating" (the devil was put on the run)? Water played a big role in writing Gospel music. "Lower Away the Life Boat," "Put Out the Life Boat," and "He Threw Out the Life Line to Me" were also in the same hymnal. You know C. Austin Miles wrote "In the Garden," but did you know he also wrote, "In the Upper Garden" and "Strike Your Harps of Gold"?

Anyway, when you begin showing concern about the new Gospel music, remember there was a time when "Blessed Assurance," "He Lives," "Rescue the Perishing," and "I Love to Tell the Story" were new and progressive. I must admit my favorite is still "Drop Kick Me, Jesus, Through the Goalposts of Life."

Remember Any of These?

A good friend of mine periodically writes a column called, "Dearie, Do You Remember When?" It's based on the old song of the same title. I've asked his permission to use his format, so here goes...

Dearie, do you remember...when "turkey" referred to a bird you ate at Thanksgiving? Do you remember when you could go out to a farmer's field and pick out a big tom or a small hen? Remember when you would make a noise, clap your hands, or give the "gobble gobble" sound just to get the tom to strut and gobble back? (Was he ugly or what?!)

Dearie, do you remember...making giblet gravy out of the gizzard, heart, liver, or whatever? Can you see it covering the mashed potatoes, sweet potatoes, turkey and stuffing? Do you remember actually making cranberry sauce from real, fresh cranberries? (None of that canned stuff!) Remember Mom making the stuffing out of old bread crusts and adding her own special ingredients? (No stove top stuff!) Test your memory about pumpkin pie made from pumpkin you picked and cut up, with crusts that Mom made from scratch, rolled out, and placed in the pie pan?

*Dearie, can you picture...*each member of the family who wanted a particular part of the turkey, maybe a drumstick or a wing or the breast, or even the "part that went over the fence last"? One even liked to pick on the neck. Remember Dad doing the carving?

*Dearie, do you remember...*when we had plays and dressed like Pilgrims and Indians? Can you remember singing hymns in school such as "We Gather Together to Ask the Lord's Blessing" or the old popular "Over the River and Through the Woods to Grandmother's House We Go"? Can you remember actually praying a Thanksgiving prayer and thanking God for blessings on school time, even reading an appropriate scripture for the holiday? Do you remember when we read in our assemblies and in homeroom those special Bible verses about giving thanks ?

*Dearie, can you remember...*heading out to church on Wednesday night or Thursday morning, preoccupied with thoughts of the big feast, football games, family fun, and then singing "Come Ye Thankful People Come" and getting everything in perspective?

*Dearie, do you remember...*the big rivalry at the high school football game? Remember dressing up as warm as possible and still freezing while hoping it was worth the effort to see your old friends, teachers, and the Thanksgiving football classic?

*Dearie, do you remember...*when the wishbone was picked clean, the turkey was a carcass, everyone was filled to capacity, and the men headed for the couch and the women started cleaning up? Remember hearing the college football games on radio until you went to sleep in the living room?

*Dearie, do you remember...*a feeling of gratitude overtaking you as the day came to a close, and you looked around at Mom and Dad, brother and sister, and realized why they called it "Thanksgiving"?

Dearie, do you remember all this? Well, Dearie, you're much older than I!

Stinkin' Thinkin'

It was back in 1949, and I was having a conversation with my bosom buddy, Willy the Worm (they called me Dirty Dave). We were just starting high school and we were in our early teens. Willy was older, and he was my mentor in dealing with parents and teachers. I went to him for counseling about what you do when you "get caught" by an adult. What should the *modis opperandis* be when things look bad in school or at home. I can remember Willy's wise advice.

First, "When caught—deny it! Lie if necessary, but don't admit anything!"

Second, "Delay dealing with the issue—It's not that important, Mom! No big deal. I'll tell you my part of the story later." In other words, Willy said, "Stall." It gives you time to make up a good excuse or hope it will go away.

Third, now Willy paused. "Another great ploy— Blame someone else. It was Joe Dugan! It was Carmen Spina! It was Frank Krick! It wasn't me. They set me up. Those guys don't like me! It's a conspiracy of my buddies to get me!"

Fourth, if the evidence is overwhelming and you are really done in, Willy said, "Go to the next level— Mom, all the kids at school do that today. All my buddies are doing the same thing!"

Fifth, when the adults threaten with severe punishment, Willy's word was, "Confess! Throw yourself on their mercy. Plead for forgiveness. Maybe even shed a tear. Don't, I say, *don't* say you'll never do it again." (Willy was intense at this point!)

As a teenager, I was overwhelmed with Willy's logic and know-how. He continued, "It would also be nice to get some friends to tell your parents or teacher what a nice guy you are. You know, you attend Sunday school and church, you are a leader at school and an all around nice guy. Why should these adults lose sight of this just because you did one wacky thing?" (What a guy! How reasonable!)

After much thought, Willy reached for this one, "Question their ability to judge you. Put the problem back on your parents or teacher. If they hadn't been snooping around, they wouldn't have found the problem. If they had stayed off your case or out of your life, there would have been no problem."

I couldn't help but think of my mentor Willy and then think of Washington, D.C. I haven't heard from Willy lately. Maybe he's working in our nation's capital.

Dave Bailey

...But Words Will Never(?) Hurt You

Rev. Ivan Odor is not very popular as a preacher. He seems to focus on the bizarre concerns of the ministry and turns people off. At times I've tried to befriend him and be a good listener and sounding board for his most recent trivial pursuit.

"Words! Words! Dave, they are so important in communication. Words! For instance, the 'N' word (racial slur) has never been a part of my vocabulary. I don't like to hear it on the streets, in the theater, movies, at pop music festivals, or any place, period! The 'D' or 'W' word is offensive to people of Italian decent, as is the 'S' word for Latinos. Words I avoid at all costs like the 'K' word for Jewish people and the 'M' word for Irish Catholics. It has taken me most of my adult life to make sure my vocabulary is prim and proper in regards to those of other religions, races, or ethnic derivations."

"Okay, okay," I interrupted. "What's your point? You'll get no argument from me on this. In fact, I had trouble coming up with some of your words just based on the letter."

"Well, it's about time someone took up our cause," he said. "They call us WASPS...WASPS...WASPS!" Rev. Odor became more intense with each statement! "Do you know what a WASP is? Talk about derision; talk about ethnic slur! White/Anglo/Saxon/Protestant—W-A-S-P! 'Cracker' bothers me. 'Honkey' upsets me. 'Whitey' is not bad, but 'WASP' enrages me!"

Rev. Odor's face reddened and his blood pressure was close to stroke level. Then he quoted from the dictionary, "A disparaging acronym for White Anglo-Saxon Protestant, used in America since the 1960s. A wasp is a stinging insect. A waspish person is one who is easily irritated, impatient,

67

quick to be annoyed. How can people be so insensitive to how we feel? That WASP word must go! I'm writing my Congressman!"

"Now wait a minute, Ivan." I tried to inject some civility into this bizarre discussion. "Don't you realize every group has had to go through its 'word' period? Quakers were called Quakers to mock them as they quaked with the Holy Spirit. 'Shakers' was a derisive term for people who shook with the Holy Spirit, and Methodists were criticized because of their methodical ways. Even 'Christian' was a put-down term for followers of Christ. So cool out! Be a WASP with pride. Remember, you too have contributed to this country."

My words fell on unfertile soil. As he left me, he was mumbling, "I'm gonna start a WASP Pride Month. I'll write the President...maybe WASP Power!"

Watch Your Word Usage!

The English language has never been my strong suit. I had an Aunt who taught school for years with special emphasis on English. She tried to help me learn the proper way to speak and construct sentences. The English language has always been a little foreign to me; after all, I was born in New Jersey! For instance, if you answer the phone and someone asks for you, should you say, "This is he" or "This is him?" I learned to avoid this dilemma by asking, "What do you want?" or saying, "It's your nickel!"

However, I have noted in listening to other preachers that some words are difficult to understand unless we know their context. One preacher talked about the King James Virgin of the Bible. Did this mean the Bible was untouched, or did he mean version?

On another occasion, a radio preacher was upset with the distribution of condominiums in school. Well, who wouldn't be? Condoms are bad enough!

Have you ever heard a speaker refer to the hill called Mt. Cavalry? This is not a place for men mounted on horses. This is Calvary, the place of the cross.

It gets worse. A preacher should be careful when counseling his people to spend time in medication—more meditation, less medication!

Like the angels, we will fall prostate before the Lord. This leaves all the ladies out, so let's fall prostrate!

Speaking about angels, we must be careful here in writing. Note that some sing, "Hark the Herald Angles Sing." Please preacher, get the right angle when writing *angels*!

Ever have an evangelist talk about being "bored again"? "You must be bored again." Jesus was more interested in being "born again."

Can you imagine how uptight the congregation was when they found out the preacher's daughter was a lesbian and hoped to appear in a new play? She actually told close friends she was a thespian, but so much for acting.

Bishop Bailey?

My phone rang at 6:30 a.m. It was a Thursday morning after a long-awaited ecclesiastical conclave (church meeting). The call waiting attachment to my phone indicated it was my preacher friend, Rev. I.M. Kidding. What could he want at this early hour? I made a serious mistake in answering. For the next 30 minutes, I heard a review of everything that is wrong with our denomination.

He started with the abortion issue, then the gays, the Boy Scout article, then the death of evangelism, and went on to the feminist and the Sophia fiasco. My head ached at all this heavy stuff so early in the day. He almost traumatized me with his ranting and raving about a "denomination adrift in the sea of liberalism, mired in a maze of misguided mission. We have no goals, we continue to lose members, our financial base has eroded...It is time for a change!" He paused. I pondered. What was coming next?

"Dave, I want you to join me in a holy crusade, a new Reformation. I am forming the Reformed United Methodist Church, R.U.M. for short!" Totally baffled, I said, "Wait, wait, I.M.! Do you know what RUM spells? Can you imagine what the press and your adversaries will call your membership? You'll all be called RUMMIES, not an appropriate description of Methodists."

But I.M. rushed on, in the heat of desperation. "And Dave, we need a leader. A leader who will help me in the vision of Reformation. We need a conference like the one we held in Baltimore at Christmas many years ago, and I want you to be the first bishop of the Rummies and convene such a conference."

The phone dropped from my hands. I felt myself crumbling to the kitchen floor. The next thing I remembered was my wife Eileen calling my name. I was lying on the couch. She seemed to be saying, "Bishop, Bishop, wake up! Bishop, the Rummies are awaiting your leadership!" Bishop Bailey, Bishop Bailey...what a nice sound! Was I dreaming or...?

Dave Bailey

It Was Me, O Lord

The Pope has set a difficult precedent for all of us in Christian work. He has confessed the "sins of the Church" in the past and has forgiven anyone who was injurious to the Church. As I read about this, I had to call my resident "father confessor"—Rev. U.R. Forgiven. It was time for me, yes, Dave Bailey, to own up to past sins and also forgive those who had wronged me. Following is a list of past misdemeanors that I dumped on Rev. U.R. Putting this in writing will serve as a further catharsis for my evil past.

I did kill the three chickens I was tired of feeding and caring for. I lied about their natural death (age 9).

It was me who stole the grapes from the mayor's yard. I tried to pass the blame to Joey Dugan, but it was me.

I did kiss Floria Willis in the old clubhouse one night. (Not once but twice when the lights went out!) She slapped Vince Gugliamo, but it was me (age 13).

(I already feel better. Writing gives such relief.)

Next, I was faking the day they sent me home from school sick. There was no pain in my side. I just wanted time off—high school was a drag (age 15).

It was me who cut the TV cable. I wanted Uncle Charley to go to bed; he wanted to watch TV. I wanted to hug Eileen. Sorry Unc! Thanks for finally taking the hint and going to bed! (age 16)

Finally, I did steal Melvin's car and go joyriding without a license. But Tom Romansky shifted the gears while I steered. (Tom must do his own confession.)

71

Following is a shortened list of those who wronged me. It has taken all these years, but I am finally free from a desire to "get even." Rev. U.R. says, "Let it go. Forgive them." So here is an abbreviated list. I forgive:

My brothers and sisters for calling me an "accident."

Sonny Foxwell for the black eye and swollen nose he gave me, and then stealing my ice cream!

Miss Marley for keeping me after school, night after night, for detention. She later became a nun!

Ronnie Nixon for stealing my girl and taking her out in his new Mercury car.

The basketball coach for not starting me at center in college just because I was five foot seven.

And finally, my brother-in-law, who loaned me shoes for my wedding—1-1/2 sizes too small! They also went on my honeymoon.

P.S. I will be happy to hear your confession. Call me at 1-800-FOR-GIVN.

Bible Fun

Let's have some fun with the Bible. It will be necessary for you to find a King James Version for this to work.

In my daily devotions, I make a note when I come upon an unusual verse. In this issue, I have compiled a few of them for your edification. Please note the following:

A cowboy movie: Joshua 8:2 – "...lay thee an ambush for the city..."

First doctor mentioned: Genesis 50:2 – "And Joseph commanded his servants, the physicians, to embalm his father." (Is this covered by Medicare?)

Major baseball game: Exodus 19:2 – "They were come to the desert of Sinai and...pitched in the wilderness." (It was a no-hitter.)

Baldness is A-OK: Leviticus 13:40 – "And the man whose hair is fallen off his head, he is bald; yet he is good."

Gray hair is better: Proverbs 20:29 – "...the beauty of the old man is gray hair."

A little scary to be in their service: Numbers 18:28 – "...offer a heave offering..." A what? Let's all heave!

Name for Howdy Doody Time: Numbers 25:7 – "...Phinehas, the son of Eleazar..." Remember Phinehas T. Bluster?

A woman named Noah: Numbers 27:1 – "...these are the names of his daughters; Mahlah, Noah, and Hoglah, and Milcah, and Tirzah."

There were "burbs" (suburbs) in ancient Israel: Numbers 35:2 – "and ye shall give also unto the Levites suburbs for the cities round about them."

Champaign is mentioned in the Bible (not a drink): Deuteronomy 11:30 – "which dwell in the champaign over against Gilgal, beside the plains of Moreh."

A place to go to the potty (to relieve oneself): Deuteronomy 23:12 and 13.

Hemorrhoids were a curse from God: Deuteronomy 28:27 and I Samuel 5:9.

An altar was called "Ed": Joshua 22:34 – "And the children of Reuben and the children of Gad called the altar Ed."

There was a Dodo (not a bird): Judges 10:1 – "...Tola the son of Puah, the son of Dodo."

There was a salesman (door-to-door?): II Samuel 9:4 – Machir in Hebrew means salesman.

Mouth-to-mouth resuscitation: II Kings 4:34 – "And he went up, and lay upon the child, and put his mouth upon his mouth, and his eyes upon his eyes, and his hands upon his hands: and he stretched himself upon the child; and the flesh of the child waxed warm."

Road Rage: II Kings 9:20 – "...and the driving is like the driving of Jehu the son of Nimshi; for he driveth furiously."

Ambidextrous man: I Chronicles 12:2. He could shoot an arrow with the left or right hand.

Things go so bad, you "pull your hair out": Ezra 9:3 – "and plucked off the hair of my head."

Mortgages: Nehemiah 5:3 – "We have mortgaged our lands, vineyards, and houses"

Senators: Psalm 105:22 – Send the message to Washington to "...teach his senators wisdom."

Cucumbers: Isaiah 1:8 – "...a garden of cucumbers..." What, no zucchini?

Liberals (as opposed to Conservatives): Isaiah 32:8 "...The liberal deviseth liberal things, and by liberal things shall he stand."

Dave Bailey

Preacher Appreciation Month

The month of October is "Preacher Appreciation Month." It is one of a long list of special days on which to remember special people. I'm sure someone somewhere is recognizing people in other professions too that month (and Hallmark is making appropriate cards for the event).

I thought it only appropriate that I make suggestions on how to show your preacher (or other clergy) that he/she is appreciated; in this day and age, the possibilities are limitless. However, upon due consideration, I think it would be better to tell you how *not* to show appreciation.

Don't give a book on preaching, especially something with a title like, "How to Improve Your Preaching."

A year's supply of Listerine mouthwash or Ban Roll-On might be misunderstood.

The all-expenses-paid trip to Israel for "A Dig Into the Past—Archeology on the West Bank." Forget it!

It may look good on the surface, but Enron stock should definitely be deferred.

Your preacher may be very "hip" and relate to the culture, but a gift certificate to have his or her nose pierced and a tattoo of "Jesus Loves Me" are a little much.

I would also avoid the six cassette tapes on "Disciplining the Children of the Family in the Parsonage." That second one, entitled *P.K.s From Hell*, is a scorcher!

Finally, and I do hope this has been helpful, do not place your pastor's resume on the Internet. You may think it is good publicity, but he or she may think you are putting it there for another reason. Pastors can be paranoid.

Find something nice to do for your preacher, please avoid those I have listed.

Cleaning Out the Joke File

Rev. I.B. Blessed recently paid me a long overdue visit, and it seemed like a great burden had left him. He was in rare form.

"I am on a spiritual high today," he said. "Burdens have been lifted. I feel like I've been washed clean, reborn again and again."

Now you must understand that I was taken back by his newfound fervor. I.B. was not the most enthusiastic guy in the pulpit, nor in his personal conversations. In fact, most of the time he was downright boring.

"So what happened?" I asked. "Finally get saved?" I joked.

"No! No! Dave, I've cleaned out my joke file. My humor has now become politically correct. No longer will I laugh at the foibles of others. My pulpit and personal life will have all such trash eradicated."

"You mean," I asked, "You will no longer knock the Baptists?" I asked in unbelief. "It's over," he shouted with hands raised to the sky. "No more Presbyterian jokes; no more Catholic priests and Jewish rabbi jokes; no more quips about nuns or the Pope, Jehovah's Witness and their visiting, Mormons and their wives, or Amish and their buggies. It is finished!"

"No more cute ones about Moses or Noah? No more rib ticklers about hell and heaven? No more St. Peter or David jokes?"

"No! No!" he cried.

Now I was getting a little alarmed. "You mean to tell me you will no longer make Sunday school teachers, other preachers, or deacons the butt of jokes?"

"Absolutely not, Dave."

I continued my line of questioning. "No more jokes about politicians, the President, the Democrats or Republicans, the Senate and Congress?"

"No more, Dave, no more."

"How about those great ones about women's lib, atheists, the ACLU, or Rush Limbaugh?" My voice trailed off. He picked up the slack.

"Let me make myself perfectly clear. I have cleaned out my Clinton jokes, Nixon stuff, Israeli jokes, Irish, Scottish, and Italian jokes, even those making light of the French. No more humor about marriage, Viagra, in-laws or outlaws, or raising children. The remembrance of some of these causes me to repent, repent, repent! The time I laughed at other's expenses..." he stopped.

I leaned forward. The seriousness of this was sinking in. "You mean...you mean...no more Methodist jokes?"

"You've heard right, Dave." I fell back in my chair; beads of sweat covered my forehead. My pulse rate increased, and I was a man undone in shock! You see, Rev. I.B. Blessed was the source of all my jokes. Woe is me!

Celebrate!

Rev. Ivan Odor was not in a festive mood. We were both at the Christmas party we attend each year, but my greeting of "Merry Christmas" was greeted with "Yea, for a while, anyway!"

I hesitated to respond, but finally made the mistake of asking, "What do you mean by that?"

"Well," he started, "Christmas is an endangered species. It used to be we only had to worry about Santa Claus or commercialism. Now the holiday season is inundated with other religious greetings such as, "Happy Hanukkah!" By the end of November, every TV station, radio station, newspaper and magazine announce the greeting of "Happy Hanukkah!" There are greeting cards, music, and even a movie with Adam Sandler about the *Grinch Who Stole Hanukkah*. He's written a song about the 12 Days of Hanukkah, too!

"Now there's a controversy over a menorah on government property. Right there with the manger scene, we have to share a menorah. Why don't they find their own season for celebration? And all their gift-giving stuff? It's like they have to be one up on our Christmas celebration. I hear there are even Hanukkah trees in homes!"

This really wasn't a good setting or an appropriate time to listen to Ivan's concerns about Christmas, but he threw the conversation into high gear.

"Just wait. Ramadan is coming. Ramadan Greetings! Ramadan cards...Ramadan movies...Ramadan gifts. Do you know a Muslim is already complaining about a crèche in his hometown? He's offended by this Christian symbol on public property. Here we go again. First the ACLU, then the atheists, and now the Muslims! Can you imagine celebrating Christmas in Saudi Arabia? You mark my words, Dave. Next we will be saturated with information about trips to Medina and Mecca, and pilgrimages to their holy sites. The Koran will be in all the bookstores. We'll soon hear calls to prayer from the mosques, and prayer rugs will be everywhere!"

I finally had to offer a few words, "Do you still believe Jesus was God on Earth? Do you still believe Jesus is the Savior of the world? Do you still believe in His Gospel? Do you still believe He is the Way, the Truth, the Life?" Without waiting for any answers, I moved close, looked him in the eye, and said firmly, "THEN CELEBRATE!"

Christian Jihad

Many people in our nation have become obsessed with wanting information on Islam. Since September 11, 2001, the faith of Mohammed has been front-page material. In my never-ending crusade to keep our readers up to date on legitimate and illegitimate concerns, I visited a friend who studied world religion in college and graduate school. He has a handle on just about anything related to religion.

When I entered his office, he became excited about a note I had found in my shopping bag at a local supermarket. Convinced it was a terrorist warning, he pulled up the Arabic language on his computer and began to translate the note. With great concern, he discovered three statements that gave him alarm. In the reprint he translated the fourth line, "Death to Baptist infidels." Line nine was translated, "Off with the heads of Methodist Sons of Satan." And line fourteen read, "May the United States of America perish by the will of Allah."

I was aghast! I felt threatened and feared that my friend and I had stumbled upon a document that should be rushed to the CIA, FBI, or better yet, the National Council of Churches office in New York! Instead, I decided to research this further with an Arab Christian friend who speaks and writes Arabic fluently—Ben I Tellu So Much More.

"Your friend is wacky, Dave," Ben said. "First, this note is printed upside down. It is backward—a novice reprint, but if you look at it properly, it is the Old Testament hope for the final work of Jesus who will take away the sins of the world." What we had stumbled on in the Acme Supermarket bag was an attempt by an Arab Christian to get out the Word to Islamic Arabs that Jesus is the Savior.

In our paranoid state, we see a conspiracy everywhere—even in a shopping bag. It reminded me of September 11 when one of our staff recommended we close down our Thrift Shop in Cowtown because it might be next on the terrorists' list. We stayed open.

Keep witnessing about our Lord Jesus. Just make sure the material is printed so people can read it.

Spring Flings

I think the Easter Bunny was more fun before he started showing up at the mall. I've seen some strange looking bunnies having pictures taken with kids. He will never be as colorful or exciting as Santa, but there was a time when children's imaginations ran wild, and you had images of a rabbit bringing Easter baskets filled with goodies (even the green artificial grass looked real). There was no limit to the scenarios that a child's mind could create.

Can you remember how good those yellow chickens tasted? Too much sugar? Make us hyperactive? Who cared? They were awesome! I could make a meal off chocolate-covered marshmallow rabbits. More than any decorated chocolate coconut Easter egg, my heart belonged to those chickens and rabbits. Jellybeans couldn't do the job. Even dyed, hard-boiled eggs paled in comparison.

How about a new Easter suit, bonnet, pocketbook or dress? (I only went for the suit.) How about new shoes? Wow! There was nothing like getting dressed up for Easter Sunday services at church! (My, how times change.) Then, later in life, there was practice for the Easter cantata, a sunrise service at the local park, and the great anthems and hymns of Easter: "Christ the Lord is Risen!" "Up From the Grave He Arose!" and "Were You There?" I've always felt sorry for those who only know "Easter Parade." Irving Berlin was a great songwriter, but he missed the joy of the empty tomb.

Of course, there were always the flowers: tulips, hyacinths, lilies, daffodils—they never looked better than at Easter. Easter cards were few and far between, but they were usually beautiful and very meaningful to give and receive. Then, of course, there was the trip to a local cemetery to place flowers on the graves of those who had passed on. The digging in the soil, the planting of the flowers, the water—all so symbolic of New Life.

I don't know who first told me the Resurrection story. It was probably my mother, and later retold to me by a Sunday school teacher. Preachers echoed it from the pulpit—He is risen. Christ is risen, indeed! As each year passes, there are more graves to visit and more flowers to take to more places. How thankful I am that someone taught me Easter is more than a bunny, a basket, a chicken, and chocolate marshmallow eggs. I need the Good News now more than ever before. JESUS IS ALIVE, and whoever believes in Him shall never die! PRAISE GOD FOR THE EMPTY TOMB!

Two Words

Periodically, it is necessary to have lunch with my ministerial friend, Rev. Ivan Odor. He has very few friends, and I believe it is an act of love to be a good listener and confidant for an aging soldier of the cross. In many ways, it is an arduous task, but a free lunch helps compensate me for the hour away from my busy schedule. After a sip or two of my iced tea and a brief word of prayer, I settle back to listen to Ivan and his latest concerns.

"Dave, the church is becoming too formal and liturgical. I've got to get out of this—there are too many changes."

I had to interrupt. "Wait a minute, Ivan, change is inevitable. It's part of life. Can you illustrate what has you so upset?" I paused and tested my grilled cheese sandwich.

"Well," he replied, "I was in a church last month that had an eternal flame or light or something hanging over the altar. Where did that come from? Then two acolytes came in and lit the candles. They were dressed in robes. Since when did our church have acolytes? I liked the old way— when we used a pack of matches or borrowed a cigarette lighter from one of the guys who smoked. In fact, there was probably a time when we didn't have candles. And have you noticed that the sanctuary is becoming more altar-centered instead of pulpit centered? So much for the Word being central to our preaching." As Ivan became more intense, he perspired, and I thought of how he was perfectly named.

"Dave, what is it with these outfits the preachers are wearing today? Once they wore black robes. Now they are getting more fancy and changing colors for the seasons: white, red, green, purple, and yellow. And who started all this about following a liturgical calendar? Our early founding fathers are rolling over in their graves with the backward collars, colored shirts, and altar cloths to match. I feel like it's a fashion show."

By now, I had devoured half of my sandwich and two glasses of tea. The salad was great, and my mind wandered to what I'd have for dessert. But I tried to be a good counselor and stay focused.

"And how about our services?" he continued. "Responsive readings and responsive singing—it almost sounds like some Gregorian chant. And all these special responses sprayed throughout the worship? Is all this necessary? And praise choruses that go on forever. Am I on another planet?"

Obviously some of Ivan's concerns are real for all of us, but I couldn't get my mind off the pecan pie. The waitress warmed it in the microwave and put on a dip of vanilla ice cream.

"What has happened to our parsonages? Some are empty. Women are preaching in the pulpit, pastoring churches, and living away from their congregations. We have debates over gays, debates over abortion, debates over divorce and remarriage. Dave, I need a word from the Lord! I've had it! I'm too old for this stuff."

A Word from the Lord…a Word from the Lord. I searched and searched. I prayed, "Lord, give me a word," and He actually gave me two words.

"Ivan," I said, "Here are two words direct from the Lord. First, RETIRE. Second, FLORIDA!" Then I finished my pie and ice cream and headed back to the Ranch.

More Names

It is always difficult to choose a name for a child. Various forces play a role in this age-old process: culture, family, ethnicity, and good ol' chance (like drawing a name from a hat). I've noticed recently that biblical names are not as popular as they once were. My name was chosen, not because of the Bible hero, but because of a good friend of the family named David Johnson. I have since learned that David is a great choice because it means "beloved one" in the Hebrew language. (Thanks, Mom!)

If you are presently in a quandary over naming a future child, let me share with you what particular biblical names mean. Or, if you are already the recipient of such a name, I will provide a public service to translate your name from the ancient Hebrew.

Adam means "red." Moses means "from water" (a great Baptist name). Rachael means "beautiful. Rahab (the prostitute) equals "broad" (no pun intended). Naomi is a "goody"; it translates "pleasant."

Did you know Leah is becoming popular again? Remember, it means "wild cow"! Abel, for the boy in your life, is "vanity." Matthias is "a gift from God," while Daniel means "God's judge," and Jethro simply means "excellent." For the family short in stature, Paul means "little." How

84

about Sarah for a girl? It means "princess," and Esther means "star."

Mary and Miriam might be avoided. Translated from the Hebrew, they mean "rebellious." Martha might be more appropriate. It denotes "lady." Lemech isn't used much anymore and for good reason. It means "destroyer." (Sounds like a typical little boy.) Jesse means "wealthy," Job "a desert," and Benjamin "right hand." Michael is a winner. It means "like God." (My son-in-law will love that one.) For the daughter you expect to be an old maid, try Jezebel. It means "unmarried."

I hope this segment is a big help to you. Names are important. I was stuck with the nickname "Beetle" all through college. In my senior year of high school, the Beetle Bailey comic strip started. So I was saddled with that in place of Dave.

Think carefully when selecting your children's names. Remember, Deborah in the Hebrew means "bee" (a real honey). Lois is "agreeable." Julia is "downy" (like a pillow). Hannah is "graceful." And for the boys, Joseph translates to "he shall add" (maybe a future accountant). Samson means "like the sun." Luke is the "light giver." Jose, a name popular in Latin America, means "aid." Lucifer is "light bearer" (not a real popular name anywhere), and our final name for this session: Mark. Its literal translation is "hammer."

At the Ready

Rev. R.U. Ready called me just after the bombing of American sites by terrorists. He was into his "Second

Coming/End Times" mode. I was not in the best of spirits, and his call was ill timed.

"It's a sign of the end, Dave! Bin Laden is definitely the anti-Christ, and the terrorist attacks are the beginning of Daniel's Time of Sorrows."

It took all my Christian grace not to call for a Christian Jihad against Rev. Ready. He is perpetually coming up with new scenarios of earthquakes, famines, pestilence, wars, rumors of wars, etc. to inflict on his congregation his latest rapture rantings. Not that there isn't legitimate concern for studying the "signs of the times" and books of the Bible concerned with the "Escatan," but R.U. Ready spends more time on the signs than he does on the Savior.

Since World War II ended, he has established his own irrational doomsday theories. Hirohito, To-Jo, Hitler, Mussolini, Stalin, Ho Chi Min, Castro, and Arafat, just to mention a few, along with countries such as, Germany, Japan, Israel, Palestine, Korea, Vietnam, Russia, Iran, Iraq, Afghanistan are all people and nations that have been woven into his theories. I thought it was time to share with Brother Ready my favorite "end time" scripture verses.

"R.U., listen closely," I interrupted. "As soon as you hang up the phone, grab your Bible and check out these important, inspired verses. It will help settle you down and give you a broader perspective about events in history."

Matthew 24:14 – "Therefore, be ye ready, for the Son of Man cometh when you think not." Always be prepared by having a lifestyle pleasing to the Lord.

Matthew 25:17 – "Watch, for you know not the hour." In other words, keep awake spiritually.

86

Luke 19:13 – "Occupy til I come." Modern translation – keep busy! Stay active in doing good for the Lord and His people.

Luke 21:28 – "Look up. Lift up your heads. Your redemption draweth nigh." Whatever happens, keep your eyes on Him, not the individual events.

"Did you get that?" I asked, but no one was on the line. R. U. had hung up. I thought, *either he is studying my four verses, or he got bored and is out looking for more signs.*

Fractured Carols

Christmas music is unique. We enjoy the carols and some of the secular songs that have helped "to make the season bright." But there are a few popular songs I am happy did not make the local church hymnal. Consider the following Christmas classics:

I'm Getting' Nothin' for Christmas, Cause I Ain't Been Nothin' but Bad (Theologically correct, but not the best message for the season of the Savior).

Rockin' Around the Christmas Tree (Have you ever tried to "rock" around a Christmas tree?)

Grandmom Got Run Over by a Reindeer (I'm not sure who this is most offensive to – Grandmom, the reindeer, or the message of Christmas.)

All I Want for Christmas Is My Two Front Teeth
(This was cute, but eventually you wanted to replace every tooth in the kids' mouth.)

Then, of course, there are the Christmas carols and pop songs that are misunderstood and mis-sung:
"While Shepherds Washed Their Socks by Night"
"Round John Virgin" in Silent Night
"Deck the Halls with Poison Ivy"
"Chestnut Roasting on an Opened Friar" (ugh)
"Angles We Have Heard on High"
Is it "I Wonder as I Wander," or "I Wander as I Wonder?"

Well, whatever you sing and whatever songs you enjoy listening to, this carol (We Three Kings) still blesses me:
Star of wonder,
Star of night.
Star with royal beauty bright;
Westward leading,
Still proceeding,
Guide us to Thy perfect light.

Weddings

Have you been to a wedding lately? I have performed a number of marriage ceremonies over the years, but when I go strictly as a guest, I am intrigued with a number of dramatic changes taking place. My good buddy, Rev. I.B.

Blessed, has also noted these changes and called to tell me of just a few he has witnessed lately.

Stretch limos—what would a wedding be without them? He recently attended a wedding with two of them at $400 apiece.

Tuxedos—the male of the species is trying to outdo the female. Basic black, gray, or white is now complemented with all the colors of the rainbow.

Music—periodically, a couple will remember this is a worship service and include God in the lyrics. Many times the songs are from the Top 40 rock station, and they forget "The Rock."

White wedding gowns—my buddy was reporting on pregnant brides wearing white, and brides who are getting remarried (sometimes for the third time) still wearing white gowns. Does anyone stop and ask, "What is white supposed to symbolize?"

Photographers—the digital cameras have added a thrilling new dimension to wedding ceremonies with everyone filming their own version for the bride and groom.

The Reception—"Do you know," I.B. asked me, "that most couples today pick out the place for their reception before setting a date or getting a minister?"

After Rev. I.B. Blessed's long tirade, I had one statement to make: "Why complain, certainly with all these expenses they are giving a much bigger honorarium to the minister now!"

I.B. said he couldn't talk anymore. (I wasn't sure if he was laughing or crying hysterically.) To help make ends meet, he was driving the limo, delivering flowers, and taking pictures at the next wedding. The honorarium for the wedding was to be $25 for the preacher.

If the Church Were Run Like Washington

Can you imagine the local church you attend being run like Washington, D.C. is? Just think of it. Every four years you'd elect a new pastor, who in turn would make all new appointments such as choir director, organist, and deacons. The pastor would have to campaign for his job and compete with other worthy opponents in a primary election.

Everything the pastor wanted to do would have to be approved by the duly elected Board of Elders. They also would be elected for two to six year terms and have their own agenda for evangelism, missions, youth, and finances—an agenda that would sometimes be in conflict with their pastor's.

Sermons would be closely scrutinized by the local congregation and local press. The news media would all carefully evaluate whatever the preacher said, how he said it, and its impact on the community. Even the performance of the choir, the organist, soloists, and special programs would be evaluated by a corps of critics.

Every week there would be reports given on attendance at worship service, Bible studies, youth meetings and Sunday school. All these would be compared with statistics from the previous week, month, and year. Finances would be a major concern and charts would flow from the computers, stressing accountability for donations to the Lord's work.

The pastor's wife and family would also be carefully watched. Can the wife play the piano? Is she friendly? Is she trying to run the church? How does she dress and what about her make-up? Are the children an embarrassment to the church? Are they an asset or a liability to the ministry? If there are negative aspects of the marriage, how do we handle them in the press? Just imagine the headlines: "Pastor and Wife Differ on the Covered Dish for Family Night," or "Pastor's Children Refuse To Sing in Choir." There would be no end to the saucy material.

There would, of course, be a positive side. If after four years, church attendance declined, finances shrunk, and problems increased, you could always use the great equalizer of democracy and vote him out!

Evaluation

Have you been to a church conference recently? I just returned from one. It was my annual pilgrimage to our denomination's "blast at the beach." Conferences, by definition, are times to confer, evaluate, report, and inspire. Unfortunately, they can also be times to bore, frustrate, and make one ask, "What am I doing here?"

Conferences date way back in church history. The first one (as reported in Acts) must have been a real winner. Controversy raged on about issues like circumcision and dietary laws. (Thank God these were not on our agenda recently.) In that first church conference, there was a great deal of division among some pretty big hitters of the faith. Decisions from that meeting in Jerusalem had quite an impact on the future of the Church.

Our conference, on the other hand, was not quite as eventful. Our most heated debate was about studying homosexuality and the church's ministry to gays. (Next year it is rumored we will set up study groups for dealing with adulterers, prostitutes, and transvestites.)

I have decided to have my sidekick, Rev. I.B. Blessed evaluate the conference and grade it as one would an ice skater or gymnast in the Olympics, from 1-10. See how this compares with your annual meeting.

> Music (congregational singing) – 9
> Music (special guests) – 8+
> Music (organist) – loud but still an 8+
> Offerings (preachers, generally speaking, are poor givers) – 6
> Morning devotional talks (Bishop really did well for that time of day. He delivered great content and delivered it well.) – 9
> Superintendent reports (Winner of The Eutychus Award—Eutychus fell asleep listening to Paul) – ZZZ+
> General reports from every board, committee, and organization in the known world – 5+
> Evening program – it got so bad that my friend didn't stay and could offer no legitimate grade. (The Shore Bore)
> Food and room – (you thought we forgot) – 9
> Fellowship with the delegates – 9+
> Beach time (time apart for devotion) – 10+

Obviously my friend is only one voice crying in the wilderness. He hopes that he will be heard so that next year he can come home from Conference inspired, not tired. Meanwhile, he is back at the beach enjoying more 10s.

Understanding Parents

Recently we came upon some excellent tips to help teenagers better understand their parents. Please place these in a conspicuous place so teenagers will see them.

Don't shy away from speaking their language. Try some strange sounding words like "let me help you with the dishes," or "yes."

Try to understand their music. Play the "Carpenters" or a gospel hymn on the stereo until you get accustomed to the sound.

Be patient with their weaknesses. If you catch your mom sneaking a candy bar, don't jump all over her. Quietly set a good example.

Encourage your parents to talk about their problems. Keep in mind that things like earning a living or paying off the mortgage are important to them.

Be tolerant of their appearance. When your father gets a haircut, don't try to hide him from your friends. Remember, it's important to him to look like his peers.

If they do something you think is wrong, let them know that you dislike their behavior, not them.

Above all, remember they are parents. It is a phase that they are going through. You will soon leave the nest and may one day have to take care of them.

Pray for your parents. They really need the Lord to get them through the difficult years of raising children.

Sports Quotes

My son was once given a book entitled, *The Bathroom Sports Quote Book: Thoughts From the Throne—Wit and Wisdom From the World of Sports.* It ended up as part of my summer reading. Please do not ask where I read it.

I found the quotes to contain some much needed humor in a summer devoid of much good news. Maybe they will lift your spirits and make you smile:

Baseball is like church. Many attend. Few understand. *—Leo Durocher*

Nobody roots for Goliath. *—Wilt Chamberlain*

Prayer never works for me on the golf course. I think it has something to do with my being a terrible putter. *—Billy Graham*

Always go to other people's funerals, otherwise they won't come to yours. *—Yogi Berra*

Everybody wants to go to heaven, but nobody wants to die. *—Joe Louis*

If God had intended man for racing, He would have given him four legs like a horse. *—Red Smith*

One loss is good for the soul. Too many losses are not good for the coach. —*Knute Rockne*

The Good Lord was good to me. He gave me a strong body, a good right arm, and a weak mind. —*Dizzy Dean*

Putting lights in Wrigley Field is like putting aluminum siding on the Sistine Chapel. —*Columnist Roger Sovior*

Your Holiness, I'm Joseph Medwick. I used to be a Cardinal. (Former Cardinal outfielder on being introduced to the Pope)

And finally, one more Yogi Berra classic: If the people don't want to come out to church, nobody's gonna stop them.

Who Would Have Thought?

When I was in grammar school, a young lady from our church traveled with me to various functions, and we sang a few duets. We were considered entertainment (some wondered why). Dressing up in the fashion of the Gay Nineties, we would open up the program with a song called, "You're Much Older Than I." The opening line asked the audience, "Dearie, Do You Remember When...?" (Earlier I had mentioned a friend who wrote a column using this concept.)

I was thinking about that old song we sang back in the 40s. I didn't have much to remember as a preteen, but now I do. Little did I realize at that time the changes I would live to see in our society, in our country, and in the church. Let me give you a few examples.

Who would have thought there would be...

A debate about God being male or female?

Hymns being removed from hymnals to be politically correct?

Ministers divorcing at an alarming rate?

Priests being charged with child molestation?

Television and radio ministries collapsing?

A nation divided over abortion, gays in the military, and gays in the pulpit?

Frontal and rear nudity so widely accepted in motion pictures, along with lovemaking that leaves nothing to the imagination, and vulgarity that is justified as "the language of the streets"?

The Phillies starting a season with a 10-3 record? (I had to throw that one in.)

By the way, the song I mentioned at the start contained the following phrase: "Dearie, if you remember, then you are much older than, much, much older than I." It is hard to believe there will be a day when people will look back and think of these as the "Good Old Days." I guess I am getting old.

Reputation by Degrees

We live in the age of education. One way to impress people is to cite the number of degrees listed after our name. I received a mailing recently in which someone had CFRE after his name (a fundraiser); a financial planner had

I do believe you are the first one in our family to graduate SIGNA-PHI-NOTHING.

CLU, CLFC, and RFU; a theologian had a LL.D. after his name I call this "gaining a reputation by degrees."

My good buddy, Dr. Knot A. Clue, stopped by the other day, and we were reviewing this phenomenon. In the course of our conversation, he gave me the old standard, "You know, Dave, what B.S. stands for? Well, M.S. is more of the same stuff, and Ph.D. is piled higher and deeper."

I politely laughed, remembering how many time I've used and heard that one. Not to be outdone, I said, "Well, some have said that Ph.D. stands for Post Hole Digger." He didn't respond as well as I had—not even a chuckle.

A few years ago, a friend in the ministry got in trouble with his D.S. (District Superintendent in the Methodist church). The preacher had never gone to seminary or college but was an excellent local pastor. He made the grievous error of putting B.A. after his name on the church signboard. When scolded by the D.S. for this inaccuracy, he responded, "Marvin, I don't mean Bachelor of Arts, I mean Joe Uncle, Born Again!"

Dr. Clue thoroughly agreed with my friend. He said, "There are the important degrees: B.A. (born again); S.F. (spirit filled); B.B. (blood bought) and S.B.G. (saved by grace)."

I got caught up in the euphoria of the moment and added, "How about C.O.G. (child of God)?"

"Now you've got it!" Knot A. Clue added. "Keep working on it!"

Dave Bailey

Taking a Stand

Rev. Knot A. Clue has decided to take a stand. He is a crusader, and since his ordination, he has been on the cutting edge of societal evolution. Now his main goal is to drag the Church into the 21st century kicking and screaming.

"It's time we stop dwelling on sin and sinners, and present the Savior!" he said. "There are millions of people who have been marginalized in the Church because of traditionalists."

I was intrigued. "Please continue Knot! I am an old dog, but I can always learn new tricks."

"Here are some of the major components of my agenda," he shot back. Fire was in his eyes!

"Multiple marriages: one man or woman with 2,3,4...whatever spouses! It would cut down on the number of houses we need, along with lawnmowers, insurance policies, etc. It is the wave of the future. (Maybe Joseph Smith was a genius.)

"Churches just for felons convicted of everything from petty larceny to murder. For too long the Church has taken a stand against stealing and killing. Who needs prisons that have become a part of the penal industry? My agenda calls for houses of worship to replace the big house."

Rev. Knot A. Clue paused here and looked at me. "You know that these people are not responsible for their deeds. Their lifestyle is greatly misunderstood. Remember we will not be a transforming congregation. We are not out to change, but to accept people for who they are. Amen? Maybe we could call this a reconciling congregation. What do you think of that?" I didn't respond only because I was trying to sort all this out in my mind.

"Now I want to continue," said Knot A. Clue. "Listen

99

closely—there's more. Why does this world deal so critically with sexual promiscuity? Can't we grow up and accept differences? Not all of us can be heterosexual. Not all of us can be monogamous. The Church needs to accept 'live-in coupling' and forget that shacking up stuff!"

He paused, thank God. I was exhausted. *Where is this guy coming from?* I just wanted this conversation to end, and I needed a breath of fresh air.

But Knot would not let up. "Finally," said the Rev. Clue, "Drug Dealers need us. Prostitutes need us. Where can they go to worship and still have their own lifestyle? Have you ever thought about the number of wife and child abusers who need refuge from the storms of life? They are probably tired out from all their abusing. Beating up someone is a strain. Hatred abounds in this culture. Much of it is stems from antiquated interpretations of the Bible. There are good and noble racists out there, even church burners, who have no place to call church home!"

What? I was dumfounded. I thought, *He's lost it – He's pulling my chain. This is a charade!*

Perspiring and shaking, Rev. Knot A. Clue took out a ballot he had prepared. "I'm sending this to every major denomination in our nation. I want these matters discussed at their next annual meeting. It can start with committees, then meetings in the local church. We can set up study groups. Then votes can be taken, and you will be the first to sign my ballot."

He handed me a pen and the ballot. The next thing I remember was waking up in the ICU.

Dave Bailey

The Search for Morality on TV!

Janet Jackson did more for the voice of morality in America than all the TV/radio evangelists and preachers combined. You all have heard the story. Some of you were eyewitnesses to the Super Bowl half-time event: "The Great Exposure!" Initial reports indicate that CBS received over 200,000 angry e-mail messages. Most were from families whose children were watching as a family on Super Bowl Sunday. My wife and I (avid Philadelphia Eagles fans still in a state of depression) had tuned out about three minutes into the half-time festivities and had moved to cable news. The opening music and action gave us an idea where the event was going, so we were out of there until football resumed.

I have read three articles since then, heard commentators, and listened to friends, all of whom were distressed by the action of Janet and co-performer Justin Timberlake (you know, the guy who said there was a "wardrobe malfunction"). In many ways, this is good news. It may begin to bring back some sanity to TV. But, give me a break. That "coming out party" showed a tiny fraction of the decline and decay of contemporary TV. CBS, NBC, ABC, and the cable networks should be deluged every day by an aroused public calling for them to censor and police what they are giving us in the name of entertainment. Janet Jackson pushed the envelope over the edge. Of course, I thought Madonna and Britney Spears beat her to the punch. (Thank God I missed that one, too.)

Those of you who are morally and spiritually outraged by the mass media, be prepared for the backlash. It's already begun. The spin will begin with the question, "What's all the fuss?" and we will soon be back to all the old routines. In seminary we used to debate the question, "Should

101

the media give us what we want or what we need?" In other words, shall the media appeal to our base senses or help us move to a higher level? Forty years later, I know where the media has come down on that question! Thank God for the off button and channel surfer. It takes some searching, but there are some redeeming programs out there.

A Passion About "The Passion"

The dinner conversation was genteel, with all the social graces expected from a group of mature adults who worship together, break bread at covered dish dinners, and even enjoy social events like the theater. But things turned sour when my good friend Cecil B. DeFame became a self-appointed movie critic.

"What did you think of *The Passion*?" my wife asked. "You know, Mel Gibson's film."

That started the avalanche of discussion, or should I say Cecil's monologue of negativity. "It was too biased," he roared. Well, that was not news for any of us. We had all heard the litany of concern about the film, but we were not prepared for the direction in which Cecil wanted to take us. "Let me tell you in just three minutes what I found offensive about *The Passion*."

"First, it was humorless—totally devoid of any good laughs. Why couldn't Gibson lighten up? Then there was the anti-Italian bias. Didn't he know that Rome was the forerunner of modern Italy? The nasty guys with whips were Romans. Bad taste to trash a whole country. Additionally, the movie was anti-military. Not one soldier was presented in a positive light. Not one! Couldn't there have been one who had a redemptive part? Come on, Mel. Did you notice it was also anti-English? English, the language of the world, was not once uttered. Language bias, that's what we call it. Hebrew and Aramaic—good grief! This is America! We speak English!"

Two couples left hurriedly at this point, but Cecil B. DeFame, noted film critic (ha!) rolled into high gear. "It was also anti-male. Men were depicted as animals, instigators of evil with duplicity in their veins. The women were all caring, all loving, and all fictional. Where is the balance? Need I mention it was also anti-Caucasian? A putdown to the white race. All the characters were white. Even Simon the Cyrene looked white, and by tradition he was supposed to be black!"

Cecil paused long enough for me to grab coats for the remaining guests and start the pleasantries of "Good night, see you later. God bless."

Cecil's wife looked dismayed, realizing the monologue would continue in the car all the way home. As they climbed into their car, I could hear those final words: "It was pro-women, pro-violence..."

Finally the car door slammed shut. Silence. Amen! Eileen looked at me, and I looked at her as we finished clearing the table. "Maybe we better go see the movie again. We missed all that!"

Attacking Angels Unaware

Recently I was at the checkout counter in our super-market when a headline on a magazine caught my attention: "Angel Shot Down Over Iraq!" It looked like an intriguing story, but I fought the urge to lay down $2 in order to read this article of universal proportions. "An angel shot down over Iraq..." Was it a good angel or a bad (fallen) angel? More importantly, who was guilty of shooting down an angel? Congress really should hold an investigation or, as they say, "a Congressional inquiry. Think of it—an angel shot down over Iraq!

Serious questions arise. Did our troops do this? How high up in the chain of command did this go? Were our troops properly trained on how to respond to seeing an angel in a war zone? Could the angel have been shot by the insurgents? Isn't this against Muslim beliefs? Had the angel come from a mosque where it was seeking sanctuary? Will this become a political issue in the presidential election? Could it be a church/state issue? Would the ACLU represent the angel if it sued the USA?

Then I switched mental gears, and thought of the major TV networks, talk radio stations, and the weekend talking head shows. Could FOX present a fair and balanced report on this one? Would Rush Limbaugh or Shawn Hannity give it a right wing spin? Would Larry King want to interview the angel? Would Michael Moore want to do a movie blaming our policy on Iraq for the killing of innocent angels?

Piling my groceries into the car, I suddenly weakened and returned to the checkout counter. I bought the maga-zine since I felt that more information was needed. Two dol-lars was a small price to pay for that knowledge. I raced home and went into my study to devour the story paragraph by paragraph. The angel, in its injured state, was rushed to a veterinarian. Yes, a vet! The vet operated on its partially wounded wing, repaired the damage, and after a few days of recuperation, the angel returned to its heavenly duty. Was it an American vet or an Iraqi vet? Unfortunately, the answer was not available. Suffice it to say I believe a dedicated veterinarian has saved America yet another international incident. Thank God for dedicated journalists who report news even when it could denigrate our great nation.

By the way, the magazine promised another terrific article next month—"Osama bin Laden Abducted by Martians: America Fails Again." I can't wait to go shopping.

Get a Life!

While watching the national conventions, it suddenly became quite clear that I would never be elected President of the United States. First the odds would be against me professionally as I am not a lawyer. Being a lawyer does seem to be a prerequisite today for those seeking public office. My research indicates there was only one evangelist (part-time) ever elected to the Presidency. By the way, he even conducted a few services while in office. Any idea who?

Next, I am not a graduate of an Ivy League school or other major university. My college just recently changed its name, thus no one would be impressed with my academic credentials. Both seminaries I attended have also closed down (one is now a Burn Center). In addition, I have little money, and most of my friends are in the same financial straits. I knew one millionaire, but he's dead, and he left his money to a ministry other than Ranch Hope. I also don't belong to the NRA. As for my political party identification, I have been neutered. Raised a strict Democrat with pictures of FDR in the home, I felt the party left me years ago. On social issues I find myself a Republican, but I part company with the GOP sometimes, too.

So I do not expect to be drafted in the near future to run for any political office, especially President. But I do have a great keynote address ready, just in case. It will call for a time of national repentance, revival, and prayer, and during the convention, I will give an altar call for the delegates to come forward and receive the Lord as their personal Savior.

Dream on, Bailey, get real! You just stepped down as Executive Director of the Ranch, and now you're fantasizing! Get a life!

More Thoughts on Father...

On Father's Day I found myself again remembering my dad, Clarence Salathiel Bailey, Sr. Dad has been gone from this earth for over 34 years. Much like every father-son relationship, there are things I'd like to forget, but many memories give me great delight.

Things to forget:

> The time he discovered me hopping cars in a snowstorm (holding onto the bumper of a car while on a sled.)

Catching me between his legs as I fled after back talking to Mother.

His long letter to me at college warning me that I was getting too serious about my girlfriend, Eileen. Seven pages, handwritten with one word—THINK! (So I thought, and the next year Eileen and I got married.)

The time I ran over our dog while I was leaving the driveway in the backyard. (He was really upset!)

A horrible confrontation about what to do after school each day. He wanted me to help him work. I wanted to watch TV's Bandstand or play touch football. (Talk about a generation gap!)

Shifting gears, I also remember the more pleasant experiences:

Trips in the old Chevy pickup buying chickens, turkeys, ducks, and eggs for resale.

Working in the garden (ugh) growing pole limas, corn, tomatoes, etc., and then selling them door-to-door.

Going to a Phillies game at Shibe Park. I still remember the Phillies beat the New York Giants 4-3!

A trip to see the Barnum and Bailey Circus under the big top tent in Philadelphia.

Watching my parents play pinochle with friends as he rubbed the cards for luck.

The summer he competed in a local newspaper contest and won $500 to help me start college after he had taken a disability retirement from the Dupont plant.

The summer when I was away near Pittsburgh, and he cut out articles on the Phillies and mailed them to me.

His coming to hear me preach and our talks about faith in God, knowing he listened to my radio broadcast. (In fact, he had just listened the morning of his passing.) Thanks, Dad.

A Prince of a Horse

Bye, bye Prince. Roy Rogers stuffed Trigger, and I thought of doing the same to Prince. Prince was the first horse donated to Ranch Hope. Way back in 1963, a couple from Vineland called and said they had a young unbroken stallion they would like to donate. Totally ignorant of what this meant and filled with anticipation, I borrowed a truck and went to pick up the donation. The Ranch needed a horse: After all, what's a ranch without a horse?

On a cold November afternoon, I arrived in Vineland, met the couple, and was introduced to Prince. After cordial greetings were exchanged, we started to load him onto the truck. Two hours later, we gave up. He would not go up the wooden ramp.

"Give me a month. I'll train him to walk up a ramp. Just give me a call after Christmas," my exhausted donor explained. So I did, and in early January, with the same truck, I headed back for our first horse. Within minutes of my arrival, Prince was tied securely in the back of the truck, and after many thanks, I headed back to the Ranch. Three hours later, I was still trying to get the horse off the truck! Such was my beginning with Prince.

Just two years after receiving Prince, he was in a serious automobile accident in which my own horse, Lucky, was killed along with two Shetland ponies. For six months I nursed Prince back to health, and we bonded forever. Now, 35 years later, he was buried at the Ranch after many years of faithful service to the boys and myself. We calculated his age to have been over 37 years. In human years he would have been almost 100.

Thanks to Howard Gruber, who helped break the young stallion for me, and to Bonnie Sterman, the first rider to finally stay in the saddle.

If there are horses in heaven, I'll just say, "Happy Trails ole buddy. We had a great ride."

Thanksgiving Memories

I was having my hair cut by an old Italian friend, A. Claus Shave, and we were reminiscing about the "good ole days." The conversation turned to Thanksgiving and days past. It's interesting how our reasons for being thankful change over the years. See if you can relate to the progression.

I'm thankful for parents; my conception (during March of 1935); my fetal period (in the 30s I was still considered a baby in the womb); my birth on November 12, 1935; my sister "Ducky" being my surrogate mom while my mother was sick; being spoiled by older brothers and sisters; a cold water baptism (Methodist style); Sunday school; church;

starting school; weekends; and friends like Joey Dugan (Yo, Joey! Can you come out and play?) Thank you, Lord.

Remember hide 'n' seek, winning at sports, Christmas and birthday parties? Can you remember your first tricycle, two-wheeler, roller skates, marbles, Monopoly set, tinker toys, and baseball mitt? Can you remember the War and praying for brothers and sisters to come home safely? Or your first dance, first date, first steady, and the prom?

Thanks, Lord, for a driver's license, my dad's truck, a job delivering papers, a job working at the movie theater, for allowing me to meet and get serious with Eileen, for high school graduation, for the opportunity to go to college, for letters from home (especially from Eileen), for a call to the ministry (more like a shout), for my marriage, and for a three-day honeymoon to Atlantic City (1956).

Thanks for the first church, seminary days, the first child (then two more), for the privilege of being on radio, for the Ranch, and for helping me raise children who became teenagers (with a special thank you that the teenage years are over!). Now thanks for grandchildren, Social Security, health, the aging process, 50 years of marriage, and the anticipation of heaven.

It's funny how what we are thankful for changes, but to whom we're thankful never does.

Praise God from whom all blessings flow.

Athletes and All That Jazz

A country western song a few years ago advised parents, "Don't let your babies grow up to be cowboys." Today someone should write a sequel to that and state, "Make sure your children grow up to be athletes." This is especially true if you are concerned about their financial well-being.

One wise sage gave a thought-provoking analysis of our perverted culture when it comes to salaries. A social worker helping inner city youth is paid $15,000 a year; a TV producer who does a documentary about the social worker and the inner city youth will receive $125,000. A teacher in the local high school responsible for educating these inner city youth receives $24,000 a year; an athlete from a pro team who comes to deliver a motivational speech to these same youth earns $2.5 million for playing 16 football games. I might add that a pastor at an inner city church, who is also trying to minister to these same young people, receives $9,000 per year. Cultural perversion indeed.

Obviously something has happened in a nation once considered the "land of the free." Nothing is free anymore, certainly not those wonderful athletic competitions once known as games. Our Lord could care less if our children grow up to be cowboys or athletes. The responsibility we have is to help our children and our society know that even in the 21st century world of athletics, "Man shall not live by salaries, bonuses, agents or TV commercials alone."

The Birds of the Field
Shall Clap Their Hands...

Jesus said in Matthew 6:26, "Behold the fowls of the air; for they sow not, neither do they reap, nor gather into barns; yet your heavenly Father feedeth them. Are ye not much better than they?"

I know that after a snowstorm, one of the things I like to do most is trudge out in the snow and clear a path to the birdfeeder and fill it up with birdseed. There is almost always a problem, and most of you know what I am going to say. Our yard is loaded with squirrels, and those squirrels play havoc with the birdfeeder.

One year I tried everything possible to outsmart the squirrels. I thought I had finally worked out a way to stop them from getting into the birdfeeder, but they climbed up the cedar tree, which had a branch that swung out just far enough that they could propel themselves like a catapult. They would jump up on the branch and swing themselves over to the other tree to get onto the birdfeeder. I finally decided to solve the problem by putting so many seeds out for the birds and so many seeds out for the squirrels because I knew the squirrels were going to be there.

Well, it is really neat to try to feed birds over the winter, and if you have a feeder, you know that dozens of birds come: cardinals, blue jays, sparrows, chickadees, finches, and titmice. They come to have a regular feast. But I wonder where they spend the night when it is so cold, what do they do when it snows and ice covers everything? I thank God that in His providence, He has provided me to help feed them. But even if Bailey wasn't around, it is amazing how the birds have a way of being provided for.

That is something good for us to remember. We provide for ourselves as much as we can, but there may come a time when we can't. We are happy that we belong to an eternal God that knows even when a sparrow falls from the sky, he is still the Great Provider.

Dave Bailey

The End Times

"News is not good," said my good friend Rev. Wor I. Wart. "Dave, have you been following the TV news, the periodicals, the newspapers? This is a tough time to be alive!" "And have you noticed all the new ways to die?" Our parents and grandparents had none of these problems. (Here I wanted to break in and remind him of all the things they did have to face).

Rev. Wart had a tic in his right eye that was very distracting; the more intense the conversations, the more intense the tic. Let me just say at this point I was very distracted!

"Dave, have you heard about the terrorist plots? They are coming up with new scenarios every day. We never had to fear this biochemical stuff before (tic, tic) or hijacking possibilities. Is travel ever going to be safe again?" (He doesn't pause long enough to breathe, let alone wait for me to answer). "Then there are car bombs to worry about or maybe a drive-by shooting as I'm coming out of church! How about poison in our water or a nuclear bomb smuggled into our country (tic, tic)? And if we get by the terrorists, there's rampant road rage! Drivers are wacky today; they might drive me off the road! Dave, I'm not losing it—the fear factor is real!"

It was now that I wanted to vaporize by whatever method was quickest, but he was relentless in pursuit of my attention.

Rev. Wart started in again. "The scientific world speculates a comet could hit us and wipe us out like the dinosaurs. Another scientist says the ozone layer is being eaten up, and soon we'll all fry in the sun" (tic, tic). (I think at this point he took some medication.) "You know, Dave, it even crosses my mind that a disgruntled parishioner, sexton, or organist could march into my office and blow me away!" (tic, tic)

I had had it. Too, too much information. Too, too much negativism. I had to leave quickly or I would need medication, the ICU at the hospital... (Tic, tic). Was that me? I quickly went to prayer and pulled out Fox's *Book of Martyrs* and Tim LaHaye's latest novel on the end times. Somehow they relieved me...tic, tic.

Memories...

It was a routine trip to my hometown, Penn Grove, New Jersey. In between two meetings, I found myself on the street that led to the Riverview Cemetery. With about 30 minutes of free time, I stopped, climbed a small incline, and visited the gravesite of my mom and dad. To be honest, I had not been there for nearly two years. Prior to this stop, I had wandered around our old homestead, which is now abandoned, boarded up, and ready for demolition. This was where I lived during high school and college, and it was the final place my parents resided before Dad died.

Looking at the yard brought back many memories. My dad and I had spent hours together planting shrubs and every flower imaginable. I looked around for any semblance of the past. (It had been nearly 50 years since we worked the yard.) Near the old garage, I came upon a row of daffodils just about ready to bloom. Instantly, I wanted to dig them up and take them with me. Then I thought better. They should remain there as a memorial to a beautiful part of my life—time spent with Dad in his garden. I went up to the back steps and looked into the shed window. How many times Mom had washed the clothes using the old Maytag, just a few feet from where I peered, standing on tip toes. A Frigidaire refrigerator stood just a few feet from the Maytag and, for a moment, I could see Mom open the door and take out food for a big Sunday dinner. She was a great cook!

That will probably be the last time I visit the old homestead. Before long, it will be just an empty lot. Maybe a "For Sale" sign will be erected, and another generation will build there and raise a family. I hope they will not destroy the daffodils, so they can still grow each spring. May they always be a reminder of new life and rebirth. As I turned to leave Mom and Dad's graves, I glanced down at the memorial stone. Mom lived from 1898–1992; Dad from 1892–1962. The dashes between those dates caught my attention. I lived with each of them on their dash. Dad and I worked the garden on his dash. Mom took me to Sunday school, church, and taught me about Jesus on her dash. Jesus came to take us beyond the dash, and because He lives, we too shall live forever.

Give Me a Break—It's Christmas!

It was about a week before Christmas, and my wife and I were busy decorating the house. A phone ringing was not a welcomed interruption, especially when it turned out to be "The Grinch of South Jersey!"

"Merry Christmas, Baileys' residence," I joyfully answered.

"This is Rev. Ivan Odor," he responded. "Give me a few minutes, Dave. I need to vent." Knowing my friend, it was useless to explain this was a bad time, so I hung on, grabbed a chair, and prepared for the worst.

"Dave, I know it's Christmas, and we're approaching a new year, but I'm fed up with the garbage on the news networks, especially the cable news. Why do they keep running and rerunning the same stories?

"The Iraq War—We should have invaded Iraq/we shouldn't be involved; there were WMDs/there were no WMDs; Iraq is better off/it's worse off; we should show the dead soldiers coming home/we shouldn't show them; the President conned us/ he didn't con us. Dave, It's Christmas!

"The Democrats running for president—they debate; they attack Bush; they attack each other; they appear on Saturday Night Live; they are on with the talking heads...It's Christmas! Wait till later for all the political stuff!

"The economy—it's recovering/it's not recovering; the DOW is up/the DOW is down; the tax cuts helped/the tax cuts hurt; there is more unemployment/there is less unemployment... It's Christmas!

"Dave...Dave...Can you hear me? Dave...are you listening? Where are you?" Click.

I must admit, I had left the room and was watching *It's a Wonderful Life*, which was followed by *A Christmas Story* (the movie about the kid and the BB gun), and then, the Boston Pops' *Songs of the Season* would be on. After all...it's Christmas!

Dave Bailey

In Memory of Reggie White

Time: three days before the Super Bowl.

Topic: Reggie White and his request for time after the football game to present a "positive message."

If there was ever a time when the anti-Christian bias of the media raised its ugly head, it was then. For nearly four hours as I went in and out of my car, I listened to an orgy of bias and ignorance. Gracefully, some of the callers tried to present another view for the hosts, but such callers were demeaned or used as a platform for additional Christian bashing. The forum was a legitimate means of discussing the pros and cons of Reggie's request for airtime, but it soon deteriorated into a diatribe against religion in general, Christians in particular. Below is a list of some of the callers' comments.

"Reggie should buy time if he wants to promote his 'ministry'; he's got millions."

"He's a phony—he's only gonna' pray if Green Bay wins. His god isn't a god for the losers, only the winners."

"I'm sick of all the players praying and crossing themselves in the end zone. The NFL should fine them like they do for any other demonstrating."

"My wife goes to church; I don't. But when I was growing up, my local church printed in the bulletin each Sunday how much people gave. They were only interested in the offering plate and envelopes anyway."

"Reggie and those other zealots are trying to jam Jesus down everybody's throat. Next we'll be having a Rabbi or a Muslim (I guess that's what you call them) wanting equal time."

117

"I watch football for football, not to be preached to. Let 'em take their religion to church! What church is Reggie anyway?"

"The Bible? Everyone has his own interpretation. It was written too long ago to have any relevance today. It's just stories and myths. Who was the guy with the technicolor hair? Remember he used to hold up the sign with John 3:16 – what was that all about? Didn't you know that nut killed himself? So much for him..."

A caller then tried to explain John 3:16. The response from the host was, "Don't start quoting the Bible..." He only got to 'God so loved the world.'

There were other positive comments such as, "Reggie was smart to get free publicity." "Got out his message."

So much for a sports talk show and its balanced coverage. Reggie did get a few seconds after the game, and he did testify. Thank God neither Reggie White nor his ministry nor the work of the Lord Jesus is dependent upon secular radio or TV!"

Beetle's Buggy

Walking home from school was rarely exciting. In fact it was routine. What gave it special meaning was the additional one-half mile with my high school sweetheart, Eileen. (We later married and have celebrated over 50 years together.) This ritual took place in our senior year. As the winter weather set in, I dreamed about an automobile that would facilitate our long trip home each night. I had my driver's license for two months, but no car. Money from my paper routes, working in a news store, and other fund raisers gave me a bank account of over $2,000. The only obstacle was my father!

The money was to be saved for college, not a car. But one afternoon the temptation was too much. There on the lot was a 1935 Plymouth Coupe with three on the floor, an AM radio, white sidewalls, and even a rumble seat. I said, "Get behind me, Satan," and he did and he pushed. Without my Dad knowing it, I bought the car for $250. Insurance cost me $750, and Beetle's Buggy was born. I decided to keep it at my older sister's house (she became an accomplice in the evil deed), so Dad would never know.

Each day I would walk to my sister's house, climb into my car, and drive to school. WOW! What popularity—what notoriety! What...tragedy! It lasted six weeks and the rear end fell out. The seller had put sawdust in the crank shaft, and everything came unglued. Beetle's Buggy was hauled off to the junk yard for $25. My father almost had a coronary, and I mourned the loss of $1,000 college money. It was a teenage tragedy—my beautiful blue Plymouth in the grave yard of old cars! But for me it was a lesson in life. For six weeks I enjoyed the pleasure of forbidden fruit. My Dad recovered, and after more effort at work, the money for college was replenished. I learned that God doesn't make junk. What we do for Him and through Him doesn't end up at Joe's Auto Graveyard.

119

Feeling Older

Periodically someone sends me an email with an article on getting old, the one that begins: "You know you're getting older when…" Well, I was thinking about that subject the other day. It was a warm summer day, and I was sitting in a church where I was substituting for the pastor who was on vacation. The layman who was conducting the service mentioned that he was 60 years of age, and I thought, *I'm probably the oldest guy in this church today, and I'm feeling it.*

Looking around, I began to wonder, *What made me feel older (not ancient, just older)?*

I finally decided you know you're getting older when…

> You're the only guy with a white shirt and necktie in church.
>
> You don't know all the choruses they project on the screen ("Do Lord," "Kumbaya" and "Hallelu" are now among the missing.)
>
> Some of the hymns you sing were written by authors who are still alive: Gaither, Andrea Crouch, Amy Grant, to name a few. In the old days, the hymn writers were all dead: Bach, Fanny Crosby, and Austin Miles for instance. (I realized that I know as many people dead as I do alive—a definite sign of aging!)
>
> You know you're getting older when the King James version of the Bible is replaced by one of a multitude of translations.
>
> You remember churches were built with stained glass windows, not stages and convertible basketball courts.
>
> You remember hymns were accompanied by organs and pianos, not by keyboards, guitars, and drums.

If you think I'm old,
you should meet my father!

Preachers look like kids to you, and many are fe-males!

You know you're getting older when the churches are air conditioned and lack hand held fans donated by local morticians.

There are no pews in the church—just comfort-able chairs.

The choirs have been replaced by praise bands.

Passing the peace (shaking hands) or a major hug causes an anxiety attack.

The Good Ole Days

Periodically I run into an old friend or family member who talks about the good ole days. Boy does that age me! I came from a family of seven children and just two parents (that really makes me sound ancient). We used to have a big round kitchen table, which was the gathering place for all of us. At that time we had two stoves—one in the living room and one in the kitchen. The stove in the living room was only lit after supper when we would all rush in and turn on the radio, an old Zenith floor model. But the kitchen stove stayed fired up all day so that it was always good and warm in there.

Every once in a while relatives would visit us. Aunts, un-cles, nieces, nephews, and cousins would make their way to the Bailey home. Invariably the subject would turn to the "good ole days." My dad would talk about growing up on a farm in Virginia and the hard work it entailed, especially in the winter: every morning he had to break the ice to get water and then carry it to the barn for the cows. All of us kids could retell the story word for word and would leave the room when we knew he was starting his trip back to the farm.

Well, Dad has been gone for nearly 50 years. At our last family reunion we all got together around a big table and started telling stories about "the good ole days," but we had our own stories to tell.

"Remember the little white house out back and how cold it was in the winter and hot in the summer?"

"Remember taking a bath in the galvanized bath tub in the kitchen on Saturday night—the same tub mom used to wash clothes in on Monday morning?"

"Remember running up the stairs and jumping into a cold bed in the freezing room?"

"Remember bringing in wood in the morning to start the kitchen fire that had gone out at night?"

About halfway through the stories, I could see my children's eyes glaze over with boredom. They had heard it all before. But guess what, kids—these will be the good ole days you'll tell your kids about someday.

Great Church Pick-Up Lines

My good friend, Rev. R.U. Ready, is still single. Since undergraduate classes at Temple University, he has been seeking a lifetime mate to serve with him in ministry. After being appointed to his first rural church, he came close to matrimony with a dairy farmer's daughter and then later with a sod farmer's firstborn. Neither ultimately worked out. Now in his second pastorate, he is again giving serious chase in the singles' Sunday school class. They call the class "The Ever Ready." He thinks of them more as never ready.

Recently he asked me to evaluate some of his "ice breakers," that is, his opening sentences of conversation. In the secular world, they would be called "pick-up lines." Obviously, R.U. is not comfortable using that language. To give you an idea why he is still single, I've listed a few of his best. The following is his e-mail to me:

"Dave, I have worked and worked on these lines and now have them down to a science:

Hi, I'm R.U. Ready. Which Bible do you prefer— the King James, New King James, Living Bible, or the New American Standard?

Are you going to the church covered dish supper? If you are, could we share the macaroni casserole?

Are you pre-, post-, or a- millennial? Pre- or post-tribulation?

Hi! Have you read *The Purpose-Driven Life* or any good books from the *Left Behind* series?

So, how long have you been coming to this church? Do you come here often?

You know, I'm the pastor here, but my real love is reaching radical Muslims in the Sudan!

The parsonage here is really small—only four bedrooms. I hope to fall in love with the right girl

and fill those rooms with little Methodists!
"What do you think, Dave?"

I paused, hit the erase button on the computer, and thought, *Rev. R.U., celibacy is still considered a virtue by many. You are going to be very virtuous!*

Keeping the Sabbath

Anyone remember the Sabbath? Anyone remember when we were taught that Sunday was a very special day? Talk about a major change in our culture! Even those of us who were raised in the church and are still active have had our lifestyle changed in regards to Sunday. For instance, there was a time (in Camelot) when some of us did not:

Go to the movies on Sunday
Shop (get it done Saturday) on Sunday
Play cards on Sunday
Dance on Sunday
Play loud music in the home or outside the home on Sunday
Make loud noise when playing outside on Sunday

Sunday was about worship in the morning, Sunday school, youth meeting, and Sunday night services. It was to be a day of re-creation—not recreation!

There was an organization that actually had this as its major focus: The Sunday Guardian. Its leader struggled locally and at the state level to protect what was called the "blue laws," which prohibited the purchase of certain items on Sundays. Ocean Grove, New Jersey, was a "Sunday City" at one time. No commercial establishment was permitted to be open except restaurants and hotels. Ocean Grove didn't even permit cars to drive in the city limits on Sunday. All that has changed dramatically!

There is now no day of rest in our society. Our culture champions 24/7 work, pleasure, buying, selling, enjoying— go-go-go! Periodically we run into pockets of resistance, and they are delightful. Take a trip to Lancaster, Pennsylvania, and signs say, "This place of business is closed on Sunday." How antiquated, old fashioned, and yet how refreshing. Even the mules and Belgian horses don't work on Sunday at an Amish farm.

Genesis says that "God rested on the seventh day. He needed it. We don't think we do. Do we ever miss a quiet Sunday (without NFL football or major league baseball)? Remember when the Philadelphia Phillies couldn't start an inning after 6:00 p.m.? Why? So people could get home from the game and go to church. Remember a nice ride in the country on a Sunday afternoon or maybe a family visit? Well, I have good news. A group of theologians and business leaders are petitioning God to have an eighth day each week. They promise to faithfully keep this one holy and get some rest. Have I heard this one before?

A Long Life

Rev. Ivan Odor and I were visiting a nursing home together, and a lady being cared for had just celebrated her 105th birthday. Ivan remarked as we left her room, "Wow, that's a long time to live! Can you imagine living on earth that long?"

I thought of Methuselah in the Bible. Can you imagine living 969 years as he did? Our life spans dwarf in comparison. I couldn't let go of that thought. After Ivan Odor left me for the evening, I returned home with my mind fixed on Methuselah and all the people he saw come and go: children, grandchildren, great-great-great grandchildren, etc. Can you imagine having to develop new friends, say every 50 years. Think of all the births, weddings (imagine the cost of presents), and funerals you'd attend. Consider all the changes in clothing, food habits, and hair styles. To put Methusaleh's life in perspective, it would be the same as being born in the year 1038 and still being alive today. Now we are talking about a lot of history!

I feel important when the grandkids ask me about the 1940s or 1950s. I tell them about Pearl Harbor, the Cold War, meeting Roy Rogers, watching the Phillies play at Connie Mack Stadium, wearing white bucks, having a DA haircut, jitter-bugging, driving a 1945 Chevy truck, and listening to the Big Bands (Frankie Laine, Eddie Fisher and the Andrew Sisters). But can you imagine saying, "Oh yeah, I was there during the Middle Ages. I remember the Norsemen and Greenland and it seems like yesterday that I read about Martin Luther and his 99 theses on the door. If I reflect enough, I can call to mind the Norman invasion, going to see Chaucer and Shakespeare at different times, hearing about the Aztecs and Mayans, the Crusaders, the American Revolution, and the Civil War!" I'm exhausted just thinking about the last 969 years, let alone living them.

Want to live as long as Methuselah? Some people believe we can be put in dry ice now after our death and awakened later if the right technology is invented. But Methuselah needed none of that. Think he had any health problems? Imagine getting arthritis at 450 years old and having it for the next 519 years. Or how about dementia at 700 years old and always forgetting where the manna was!

There is a better plan for the future—eternal life with the Lord. Even Methuselah eventually died physically. We will too, even after the dry ice deal. But for me to live is Christ, and to die is gain!

The Numbers Guy

I'm always impressed with the usher who counts the members of the congregation on Sunday morning. Church after church where I preach, there is usually an usher who faithfully and meticulously does the "numbers" every week. The results of his work are usually published in the bulletin the following week. People look at the totals and can often evaluate the preacher's ability, or lack of it, to attract a crowd. These numbers are second in importance only to the financial report. Oh, the mystique of watching the ushers take an offering, return it to the altar, and after the service, take it to the office and count it. What a ministry! Counting! Numbers! Figures! Tabulations! Glory!

It dawned on me, as I was having my devotions the other morning, that some people in Bible times had to do a lot of counting. For instance, I recall reading about 150,000 soldiers of the army of Israel going to battle 300,000 soldiers of the enemy. Who did the counting? There were 75,000 men slain...ah, now that would be a ministry. Can you imagine going over the battlefield and totaling the dead one by one? There would be a part of me that would want to estimate—let's see, 1,000 here, 1,000 over there...It's an acre of land and that should hold 10,000 fallen soldiers. No need to go one by one!

Then I was reading in another part of the Bible about the animals. Noah's calculations were nothing compared to sacrifice time: 5,000 rams, 4,000 sheep, 8,000 goats, 6,000 bulls, etc. Can you imagine standing in the animal pens working these numbers? What a life! And how about Solomon's horses: 4,000 horses and chariots. That's a nice round number. How about the ministry of taking care of all the manure?

But the Bible is also clear about the numbers regarding the construction of the tabernacle. This was the place of worship, so it had to be exact—walls covered with 3,000 talents of gold, 7,000 talents of refined silver, 10,000 darics of gold, 18,000 talents of bronze, and 100,000 talents of iron. And this was before the time of calculators! There was also the ministry of counting the members of the tribes. Ezra lists all those who returned from captivity to Jerusalem. This was no small task. To God be the glory for those who went from tent to tent counting.

Of course, the New Testament has its numbers, too—like the feeding of the 5,000 and the feeding of the 4,000. (Could there be a 4% range of error?) And 3,000 souls were saved at Pentecost. Is this an evangelistic count? I know the Holy Spirit inspired the Word, so I'm sure the inspiration filtered down to the numbers. But it's fun just to speculate about who came up with the numbers.

I challenge those of you who are turned on by book-keeping and accounting (counting the jelly beans). Your ministry is important, so keep up the good work. Just remember the guy who got to heaven and bragged about living through the Johnstown Flood. Peter reminded him not to brag because Noah was nearby. So before you swell up with pride for your gift of counting, check the book of Numbers. Now that's a ministry!

Letter From an Unknown Boy and Girl

Dear Friend of Ranch Hope,

I am writing you on behalf of hundreds of unknown boys and girls who will have a home because you care. You will never know me personally. We will pass on the street and neither will recognize the other...to you I will remain an unknown. But you have now become a part of my life. Although our relationship may end with this letter, you have now affected the course of my life. You may never have me in your home, but I know you have made a place for me in your heart.

I live in a building that your support has constructed. I eat at a table you have helped provide. I sleep in a bed, play on a floor, study at a desk, relax in a chair, wash at a sink, and pray in a home your efforts have built.

Is it any wonder I want to go to each of you and enthusiastically shout, "Thank you!" Thank you for giving me the dignity of a home, instead of the isolation of a cell. Thank you for giving me the dignity of being a son or daughter, instead of being called a number. Thank you for helping those who want to reach me before I become unreachable. Thank you for caring instead of condemning. Thank you for getting involved instead of enraged. Thank you for loving me in the way that counts—by action, not just words. Thank you for every minute you pray. Thank you for every dollar you donate. And especially thank you for believing that I am worth it.

You have now become my mother, my father, my brother, my sister, my aunt, my friend...my hope, my future. For many years to come, I will see your love in the bricks and mortar, wood and glass; yes, four walls and a place to feel secure. Now I know somebody cares.

You have given me something my parents may have ignored. You have given me something that the ghetto denied me. You have given me something I dreamed about, prayed for, and cried myself to sleep about...I now have a place to call home.

God bless each of you. If anyone asks, "Is the child black?" say, "Does it really matter?" If someone asks, "Is the child really that bad?" ask them if it really matters. If they ask about us, "Are they from the city, the suburbs, the country; are they middle class, slum kids, or from the upper class?" tell them only God knows. Troubled boys and girls come from every race, religion, ethnic group, social level and section of the nation.

Just take this thought with you. A thought that echoes the words of our Lord: "Inasmuch as you have done it unto one unknown child, YOU HAVE DONE IT UNTO ME."

God bless you...I love you

(Signed) An Unknown Child

(Composed by Rev. Dave Bailey on behalf of the boys and girls of Ranch Hope and Victory House)

Acres of Diamonds

Part of my college and seminary training was spent at Temple University in Philadelphia. (Yes, there was a seminary there). The Seminary was closed in 1959 because of lack of funds. The following article made the closure even more ironic. Read on...

Dr. Russell Conwell is considered one of the most interesting Americans of the 19th century. He was born Russell Herman Conwell in 1843 and lived until 1925 (83 years). He was a lawyer 15 years before he became a clergyman.

One day a young man went to him and told him he'd like to go to college, but that he couldn't raise the tuition. Dr. Conwell decided to build a university for unfortunate, but deserving, young people. He quickly realized that such a dream also required a lot of cash...several million dollars. But for Dr. Conwell, and anyone with a burning purpose in life, nothing could stand in the way of such a goal.

Several years before this incident, Dr. Conwell was intrigued by a true story, a story with a timeless moral. The story was about a farmer who lived in Africa. Influenced by a friend, he became tremendously excited about looking for diamonds; they had been discovered in abundance on the African continent. The farmer became so excited about the idea of collecting millions of dollars worth of diamonds that he sold his farm and headed out to the diamond mine.

He wandered the continent searching for diamonds and wealth. The years slipped by and he found nothing. He became completely broke and threw himself into a creek and drowned. Meanwhile, the new owner of his farm picked up an unusual looking rock on his place. It was about the size of a yard egg; he put it on his mantle, considering it only a curiosity. A visitor stopped by and, in viewing the rock, almost went into convulsions. He told the new owner the funny looking rock on his mantle was likely the largest diamond that had ever been found. The new owner replied that his whole farm was covered with rocks like this one. This farm turned out to be the Kimberly Diamond Mine, the richest diamond mine the world has ever known. The original farmer had been standing on acres of diamonds, but he had sold his farm.

Dr. Conwell suggested that, much like the story, we are each standing on our own acres of diamonds. It is our responsibility to develop the ground we are standing on before we charge off in search of greener pastures. Dr. Conwell told this story many times and attracted enormous audiences. "Acres of Diamonds" brought in the funds to start a college for underprivileged, deserving students. In total, he raised almost six million dollars to found Temple University in Philadelphia. Russell Conwell is buried on the campus on Broad Street in Philadelphia.

I think that's all I had to say...or am I just
having a senior moment, and there's
more to tell? —Dave

About the Author

Dave Bailey founded Ranch Hope, a home for troubled youth in Alloway, New Jersey, in 1964. For more than 40 years, Ranch Hope has helped young people from throughout New Jersey and the region. Rev. Bailey continues to serve the Ranch as Director of Development.

Bailey holds a Bachelor of Arts degree from Western Maryland College (now McDaniel College), and was honored as Alumni of the Year in 2002. He earned a Bachelor Degree in Divinity and a Masters Degree in Theology from Crozier Seminary (now Colgate Rochester Divinity School). Bailey received the 2006 Community Spirit Lifetime Achievement Award for Salem County, NJ, and the 2005 Community Service Award presented by Salem Community College.

Rev. Bailey is a member of the National Association of Religious Broadcasters and is the recipient of the Percy Crawford Award for Excellence in Radio Broadcasting. He has hosted various radio programs that are heard through the northeastern United States for more than 49 years.

He is the co-author of *Hope for Dead End Kids: The Story of Ranch Hope* and is the Founder and Editor of the *Salt and Light in the News* newspaper.

Rev. Bailey and his wife, Eileen, have two children, Elizabeth and David Jr., and five grandchildren.